HORIZON

SUMMER, 1972 · VOLUME XIV, NUMBER 3

HORIZON

SUMMER, 1972 · VOLUME XIV, NUMBER 3

HORIZON is published every three months by American Heritage Publishing Co., Inc. Editorial and executive offices: 551 Fifth Avenue, New York, N.Y. 10017. Treasurer: Marjorie C. Dyer. Secretary: John C. Taylor 3rd. All correspondence about subscriptions should be addressed to: HORIZON Subscription Office, 379 West Center St., Marion, Ohio 43302.

Single copies: $6.00. Subscriptions: $20.00 per year in the U.S. and Canada; elsewhere, $21.00.

Cumulative indexes for Volumes I–V and VI–X are available at $3. HORIZON is also indexed in the *Readers' Guide to Periodical Literature.* The editors welcome contributions but can assume no responsibility for unsolicited material. Title registered U.S. Patent Office. Second-class postage paid at New York, N.Y., and at additional mailing offices.

Great Divides

British waiting to attack: July 1, 1916

To the generation that lived through it, the First World War was, and remains, the "Great War," great not in glory—for there was little glory— but great in its sheer destructive magnitude, in the unparalleled size of its armies, the unparalleled lengths of its casualty lists, and most important, in the hideous wound it inflicted on the established order of things. The Great War seemed to close an era, like some raging river sweeping away all bridges between past and future. In the current issue of HORIZON Robert Cowley pinpoints what for England may well have been the day when that fateful breach with the past occurred—July 1, 1916, the opening day of the battle of the Somme, which eventually claimed more than one million casualties. In a complex and eloquent re-creation of that battle, beginning on page 64, Cowley describes what the Somme meant to the soldiers in the field, to the generals in command, and what it meant, in the end, to England, which felt the wounds of the slaughter for a generation.

Like the Biblical Leviathan, the Great War haunted the imaginations of thoughtful men in the postwar years, among them one of the greatest of all film directors, Jean Renoir. In the 1937 film masterpiece *La Grande Illusion* Renoir gave his answer to the central question: what did the Great War portend?—an answer that, for Renoir, was bound up with the war's final destruction of the old European aristocracy. Renoir's film is described and its innovations analyzed by Stanley Kauffmann as part of his HORIZON series "Landmarks of Film History."

Perhaps the most decisive single consequence of the Great War was the Russian Revolution, which brought Lenin and the Bolsheviks to supreme power. HORIZON publishes here excerpts from a long-lost manuscript biography of young Lenin written by a fellow revolutionary, Leon Trotsky. If we think of

Lenin and Trotsky as peculiarly modern figures, Trotsky's account of Lenin's boyhood will come as a distinct surprise. It not only shows Lenin as a hardworking, hearty youth solidly rooted in a sensible, almost Victorian middle-class family, it reveals Trotsky himself as a child of the same vanished age, manfully extolling the solid virtues of hard work, healthy living, and maternal devotion. In the moral sense, most of us are far more "modern" than those two modern revolutionaries, who grew up on the other side of the war's great divide.

The idea that history is demarcated by catastrophes lies deep in man's understanding, and no catastrophe has cast a stronger spell than the story of a universal flood. Beginning on page 104 of this issue, J..W. Burrow traces the historic career of the Flood from its origins as a general Mesopotamian myth, to its central place as a historic truth revealed in Scripture, to its strange metamorphosis into a scientific doctrine—known as "catastrophism"—expounded by nineteenth-century geologists, and to its final diminuendo into a quite local disaster that occurred, archaeologists say, along the Euphrates River some six thousand years ago.

But dividing lines do not have to be catastrophic. The one with the most universal importance in human history, the Neolithic revolution, saw a change that was barely perceptible at first. As long as ten thousand years ago—in some parts of the world at least—men ceased to hunt and began to farm; they also began building cities. According to an essay by J. H. Plumb, *that* epoch is now at an end. Throughout recorded history, Dr. Plumb says, all civilizations, whatever their differences, had one fundamental feature in common: the great majority of the population tilled the soil. This is no longer true, and the various dislocations and disruptions of the twentieth century are signs of this vast social upheaval: the disappearance of men from the land. Our ancient and familiar institutions—government, religion, the family, the city, the schools—arose to accommodate a society that was chiefly agrarian. Now their usefulness has come to an end—if not for us, then certainly for our grandchildren. With what can the foundations of society be replaced? Indeed, can they be replaced? Whatever the answer, we are, according to Dr. Plumb, approaching a chasm in human history as deep and as wide as the one between man the hunter and man the planter. What awaits us on the other side of the gulf remains in doubt.   W.K.

PALAZZO MEDICI-RICCARDI, FLORENCE—SCALA

The handsome young rider on the cover, thought to represent Lorenzo de' Medici, is a figure in the fresco (left) painted by Benozzo Gozzoli in 1459 for the chapel of the Medici-Riccardi Palace in Florence. In his splendid person the horseman embodies some of the great institutions of civilized society: the state (the Florentine Republic), religion (the fresco depicts the journey of the Magi), family (the proud Medici), education (producing "the Renaissance Man"), and the city (Florence again) as the center of commerce and culture. After ten thousand years of continuous existence, says J. H. Plumb in an essay beginning on the next page, all these institutions are in peril.

An epoch that started ten thousand years ago is ending. We are involved in

a revolution of society that is as complete and as profound as the one that changed man from hunter and food gatherer to settled farmer and craftsman. Ten thousand years ago the Neolithic revolution closed an age that had lasted for hundreds of thousands of years. The foundations of society created by that revolution have endured, no matter how sophisticated and elaborate the superstructure of civilization has become. Only within the last century have these foundations begun to crumble, as the new scientific and industrial revolutions spread with ever-increasing speed throughout the world.

But how few of us realize this is so. We rage against governments, rage against churches, rage against cities, rage against schools, rage against marriage, and rage against men. Nothing seems to work, nei-

By J. H. PLUMB

ther God nor government. Science, once the great hope, is now the Hypocritical Polluter. Has this generation, we wonder, wrecked the great institutions that have molded human life for so long —family, organized religion, government? Whatever our political commitment, there lies a burden of guilt on many of us, a feeling that somehow we have lost our way, that we are responsible for the breakdown in social and private morality and in the discourse between the generations.

The problem lies deeper, locked in history, and to understand it we need to know what the Neolithic revolution did for the human race. First, it increased the food supply so that millions of men and women replaced the scattered tens of thousands of the hunting and food-gathering era. But nature is capricious, so the fertility of crops and animals became a focus of hope and fear that gave rise to elaborate rituals. At the earliest dawn of urban society organized religion is there; temples with estates to support the gods, both benign and evil, and their servants the priests.

Sometimes combined with, and sometimes distinct from, the priesthood, there are civil magistrates, lawgivers, warriors. The most magnificent relics of these early millenniums of the Neolithic revolution are the ziggurats of Sumer, Akkad, and Babylon within their fortress cities—monuments both to their gods and to their godlike kings. In Egypt the Pharaohs were god and king: they created temple cities built for eternity.

Naturally such complex societies, which arose with surprising speed once the revolution got under way, made commerce more steady and far-flung than it had been in the primitive hunting days. And increased goods, whether from far or near, required numeration. All early writing stems from the need to list and record goods. Some societies, such as the Incas, developed only a complicated knotting system, but Egypt and China and Sumer devised a pictorial shorthand that rapidly grew

into a highly complex written language. This brilliant invention released new potentialities by creating a social memory that was more reliable and exact than oral traditions could ever be. With written language the creative genius of men had an exceptional instrument. Yet this instrument was available only for an elite. From the time writing was invented until the twentieth century only a small percentage of mankind could read and write: the educated class that could be supported by societies based on agriculture and crafts was always small.

From the time writing was invented until the twentieth century only a small percentage of mankind could read and write . . .

Imperial Rome, T'ang China, the France of Louis XIV, the Mexico City of Montezuma—all the civilizations that we know are children of the Neolithic revolution, certainly each with its own striking individuality and excellence, but also with the same basic structures, the structures that we first discern in ancient Egypt and in the valley of the Tigris-Euphrates. In all these civilizations the bulk of mankind toiled on the land, struggling to wring a living from the soil that would suffice to pay taxes, make offerings to the churches, and provide a surplus to sustain a social elite. In all this economic activity the basic unit was the family: some of the more sophisticated societies evolved more complex forms of economic organization, but the family group—father, mother, children—remained the most effective social and economic unit for ten thousand years.

The masses in all societies were illiterate and poor, and this was universally regarded as a part of the natural order. As the Sumerians put it, "men are slaves of the Gods": their duty was to work. At times, in all societies, the rage of the poor broke out in sporadic violence, but the remarkable fact is not the occasional rebellion but the millenniums of docility. This was due partly to men's terror of the mysterious forces of nature that dominated their lives and that could give or deny them abundance. They needed gods, and priests and ritual, especially ritual.

Religion touched millions of men in their daily lives. Every village, every community, whether in sophisticated societies or simple ones, had its temple, its priest, its communication with the gods. For ten millenniums men have been god-haunted through all the days of their lives.

Compared with religion, the secular forms of government were less powerful socially, even though they could often dominate the structure of organized religion; in Pharaonic Egypt or imperial China they absorbed many of its functions. Most societies possessed a warrior class from which a king was selected. The warrior class also developed into a landed aristocracy, except in imperial China, where the scholar-gentry disdained the profession of arms. Elsewhere the great landowners, together with successful merchants, lawyers, priests, and government officials provided the small governing elite, which tended to breed its own successors.

Theoretically, as in China, several societies provided a system by which the talented poor might rise. In practice this very rarely happened. In the epoch that is now closing, social mobility was extremely rare. Schools and universities, like all forms of private culture, were produced by and for the elite. Schools were often rigorous and austere, designed to transmit the culture of the ruling class to the next generation of rulers. From Tibet to Ireland they were dominated by classical learning, for all societies revered the past as a storehouse of wisdom: history was used to demonstrate the divine nature of authority as well as the truth of religion, so that education was far more than learning a skill, it was the key to the understanding of life, of society, of the universal truths.

Although culture and the past belonged largely to the governing elite, there was still a need for public art, mainly monumental architecture, statuary, or descriptive pictures, that spoke of the majesty of kings or gods and helped to strengthen the social matrix that bound the governor and the governed together. The great public rituals of religion, whether it were a solemn Te Deum in Notre Dame or the dramatic human sacrifices in ancient Mexico, all forged a sense of identity between the governor and the governed. Civilization, whether primitive or advanced, was highly ceremonial.

No matter how complex these societies became, they bore a remarkable number of common features, not only in the way the majority of men and women obtained their livelihoods, but also in the structure of their institutions. Humanity was ruled by monarchs or priest-kings, there was organized religion supported by the state, there was an aristocracy of warriors and landowners. An elite of scholarly men came from these classes to serve the state or its church and maintain the authority of tradition; below them was a class of merchants whose wealth commanded special privileges but who were often at risk. The bulk of the population, however, lived in villages, tightly bred in tradition both in work and belief. Towns were small and cities few, and they were designed as centers of religion, government, crafts, and trade, sometimes one function dominating, sometimes another. And it must be stressed again that these societies were highly ceremonial, in secular as well as religious activity.

For more than ten thousand years this remained the basic pattern of human living everywhere. It began to crumble discernibly only a century or so ago. Even then such changes as occurred were very small and their significance not understood. Not until the twentieth century did it become obvious that an age-long social structure was breaking down, and not until after World War II that it was incapable of survival. Only now are there a few historians, a few sociologists, a few perceptive thinkers, who realize that we are—capitalist or communist—in the throes of a social revolution, and that the ills of our society, for which we so often assume the blame, arise from the fact that the old basic institutions are less and less suitable for the modern world. Confusion and chaos, so caused, are naturally greatest where society is freest and experimentation is permitted—in America and western Europe, for example, rather than in the communist East, where social institutions are held rigid, even though economic experimentation may possibly go deeper. The one exception may be China, where revolution has penetrated more deeply into society.

We have two epochs in conflict—an ancient system of institutions struggling with . . . a totally new economic life-style.

Let us look more closely at the revolution in which we are involved and at its consequences. It began haphazardly and, like the Neolithic revolution, went unnoticed by the world at large. In the sixteenth and seventeenth centuries a few men in western Europe began to feel a new confidence, to believe that they or their descendants might outrank the ancients in knowledge and in achievement. Slowly, science captured more and more gifted men and secured greater and greater triumphs, but to start with, it had little or no effect on society. The idea came gradually to nonscientists that experimentation was admirable in itself and should be applied to economic life. Again, this might have led nowhere, but Europe, and particularly England, had a buoyant market for goods, a plentiful supply of money, an expanding population, a wide-ranging commerce, and almost constant involvement in war—all of which stimulated production and helped bring about, at the beginning of the nineteenth century, the first stages of the Industrial Revolution.

A hundred years later the Industrial Revolution had spread throughout Europe and America, lifting mankind to a new level of civilization. Men left the countryside, until by the middle of the twentieth century the majority of people in western Europe and America were living in cities. Crafts had ceased to be of much importance, and production was now on a mass scale in large factories. The world was richer than it had ever been, although wealth was as ill distributed as it had been throughout the earlier centuries.

A great revolution in living had taken place within the institutions of the preindustrial world; but its culture, its intellectual and religious attitudes, were scarcely touched by the new world. With every decade, however, they were called into question. And so we have two epochs in conflict—an ancient system of institutions and cultures struggling with a new system of production, a totally new economic life-style. The old institutions decay, and new, more appropriate ones do not arise to replace them.

Take monarchy, the most sacred of lay institutions, one that emerged at the very dawn of recorded time: before 1900, only France, Switzerland, and a few American nations had managed to discard it. World War I shattered the world's monarchies, and World War II swept away the remains, except in two or three countries where it was saved by obstinate tradition or lucky chance. Gone are the Czars, the Kaisers, the Emperors, Kings, Serene Highnesses, Grand Dukes, and Archdukes: they linger in pathetic little exiled courts huddled about Lausanne or Estoril.

The aristocracy, that ancient warrior class whose strength had won it titles, riches, honors, and land, found itself stripped of rights, deprived of power, often slaughtered or chased into exile to exist on a pittance—often forced to work for a living. Even in England, where the monarchic tradition is strong, the power of the aristocracy was sharply diminished. Now, not even the noblemen regard themselves as a race apart, set above all others by God to advise kings and rule men. But no society has evolved anything to provide the social cohesion or the dramatic ceremonial quality once given to life by the aristocracy and monarchy.

This new revolution has attacked human institutions more fundamental than monarchy and aristocracy, for all social functions are in the grip of change. Institutions that gave these functions form and strength are now in question. Let us take four, the city, organized religion, the family, and the schools—all of these institutions have for millenniums been the matrix of society from China to Rome.

One of the first complex organizations to arise from the Neolithic revolution was the city. It provided, among other things, a vast center for religious ceremonial, as at Thebes or Chichén Itzá—which were created purely for this purpose. In many other cities the sword ruled with religion; secular and spiritual authority might be combined in the same ruler, though sometimes the two authorities remained distinct. There is no more impressive image of this duality than in the medieval cities of western Europe, where cathedral and castle sit side by side. Naturally, cities served other social purposes as well. Commerce contributed to the growth of the city, as did crafts and primitive industry, so that the city became the economic center of the surrounding countryside, a market place for local and foreign goods.

Market places were an integral part of city life. With religion in need of ritual, and with secular authority in need of power, with commerce from afar providing exotic ideas as well as goods, cities became centers of art and cultural exchange, the natural home for a scholarly elite, the home of pleasure as well as religion. They became the heart of society, a mirage that enticed the ambitious, the creative, the seeker of power. Rarely has any human institution concentrated so much within itself. This is true of Montezuma's Mexico City, Socrates' Athens, Franklin's Philadelphia, or the Goncourts' Paris.

Look at the desolate center of Detroit, with its parking lots and ghettos cut by expressways . . . Everywhere from Marseilles to Seattle cities are emptying and dying.

But, what now? Look at the desolate center of Detroit, with its parking lots and ghettos cut by expressways that hurry the bankers and merchants out of the commercial areas as quickly as possible. Everywhere from Marseilles to Seattle cities are emptying and dying. For a century now they have had no defensive value —indeed, rather the reverse. They are now targets for holocausts and are totally indefensible. Castle and city walls are merely quaint symbols of a dead past.

Nor are they the seat of organized religion, the center of dramatic ritual, the home of priest-kings or even priests. Moscow's patriarch is an active civil servant, the Mufti of Cairo is of little account, Rome is no longer the Vatican, and the Dalai Lama, the last of the priest-kings, dwells in exile. The city churches themselves can scarcely maintain an existence; with next to no congregations they steadily close. London was happy to sell a Christopher Wren church to a Missouri town.

Nor are cities essential to government. Brazil can be governed as easily from Brasília as from Rio de Janeiro; and the President of the United States can govern from Florida, California, or the Spirit of '76. If the Pentagon were removed to Death Valley and the Treasury to Boise, Idaho, the government of the most complex society on earth would not suffer.

And neither commerce nor industry needs the city. The port of London has decayed to the point of death—dock after dock has closed. The volume of New York's trade diminishes. Markets are also finished: Les Halles have been uprooted, Covent Garden closed; shopping centers, vast and complex, root themselves in suburbia where people dwell, or wish to. All that is left— and for how long?—is the world of pleasure, the restaurants, the theatres, the shops for the rich or for tourists, whether from the suburbs, the provinces, or foreign lands. The majority of commercial enterprises could move from the great cities of the Western world with no loss: improved means of communication, one of the greatest triumphs of the new industrial and scientific world, have obliterated distance and made propinquity meaningless.

It is true that swarms of men and women still flow in and out of the cities every day; no pressing social need compels them except that their offices and factories happen to be located there. Sooner or later, commerce and industry will hive off to more appropriate social situations. That the city survived as the heart of civilized life for ten thousand years is no passport for its survival in a scientific and industrial world.

But the city is still more vigorous than other institutions that are millenniums old. Organized religion, with the paraphernalia of temples, priests, and festivals, goes back to the first emergence of civilization as we know it, but that, too, is now only a shadow of what it was. In England, where, oddly enough, the decay of organized religion may have gone farthest, congregations at village churches are often under ten people. Chapels, the homes of vigorous dissenting groups in the nineteenth century—Methodists, Baptists, Congregationalists, and the rest —are no better off.

The strongest church in the world— the Roman Catholic—is in convulsions, weakened by a declining priesthood and rent by a new radicalism. The dissolution of organized religion is further reflected in the growth of half-baked mysticism, the dabbling in magic and astrology, the spread of Buddhism and Christ cults among the middle-class young. The impulse to believe still runs strong in many young men and women, but they cannot accept the forms in which belief has been encased for centuries. Religion may persist, but what are unlikely to remain are the institutional manifestations that were a part of the secular structure of society.

Equally as interesting as the decay of formal, organized, church-structured religion is the new confusion of belief: the way the sexual revolution has spread like measles through religion. Roman Catholic priests and nuns demand the right to marry so that, of all things, they can be fulfilled as human beings; the Anglican Church cautiously commends extramarital relations and without much reluctance, accepts lesbianism and homosexuality; the Quakers, at least in England, accept the entire sexual revolution so long as love dominates. Strict belief in the Christian myth is no longer necessary when an Anglican bishop can state publicly that God is dead. Any clergyman of half a century ago, no matter what denomination he belonged to, would be appalled by the state of organized religion today. He would be as baffled as an eighteenth-century connoisseur of art confronted by a Jasper Johns.

For religion is not alone in collapsing into near anarchy—the same is true of all the arts. Painting, sculpture, music, poetry, and a great deal else would be incomprehensible to a cultured man of the nineteenth century; whereas an artistically inclined Greek of the fourth century B.C., or an Egyptian of 2000 B.C., or a mandarin of Han China would have had little difficulty in appreciating to the full the poetry, the painting, the sculpture, and the literature of the nineteenth century.

Roman Catholic priests
and nuns demand
the right to marry so that,
of all things,
they can be fulfilled as
human beings . . .

The new social revolution penetrates deeper, far deeper, than this, into the very basis of society and its primary institution, the family. For ten thousand years and probably longer, but certainly for as long as we can discern, the family has been the basis of society, its most powerful social and economic unit. In most agrarian societies husband-wife-children grouped in a family are an adequate self-supporting work unit, in which there are carefully differentiated and accepted divisions of labor.

The family, of course, was far more than an economic unit. It was a school that provided not only technical education, but education for life. Most of humanity throughout history never went to any other school. It was in the family that boys and girls learned their skills as farmers or craftsmen or housekeepers. As they learned, children received also from their fathers and mothers the social morality—their attitudes to secular government as well as to sexual morals. With all human institutions the family had its crashing failures as well as its successes, but it was a highly complex and powerful institution, through which all human beings in all centuries of settled agrarian life had to pass.

Now the economic and social function of the family is rapidly breaking down—it no longer teaches economic skills and social morality. Schools and society at large have absorbed these functions, with the result that the family is now so reduced in social and economic function that it breaks down very easily under its material stresses. In the past, of course, men and women often grew to hate each other in marriage, or to be bored, but the social and economic bonds were so strong that in most societies divorce was unthinkable. A man might take concubines or other wives, and in a few idiosyncratic societies a wife might take lovers, but although a few societies permitted easy divorce, they were very rare. In advanced or developed societies divorce, except for the very rich and powerful, was almost impossible. But now the social and economic weakness of family life is demonstrated by the steady increase in divorce and the growing acceptance of men and women living together without marriage at all.

In the care and protection of children the family still performs an important function that society as yet cannot easily replace, but the education of children no longer takes place within it. Schools themselves, however, are in little better shape than families, organized religion, or cities. There is a powerful radical movement to de-school education; indeed schools are constantly being denounced as prisons and concentration camps. "The belief that a highly industrialized society," writes Paul Goodman, "requires twelve or twenty years of prior processing of the young is an illusion or a hoax." Pupils denounce curricula as irrelevant, and schoolmasters themselves have little faith in what they teach, if one can judge by the constant soul-searching and debate that accompany any conference of teachers. And yet more and more pupils are pressed into the system for longer and longer. Unhappy, frustrated, disoriented, not only do college campuses flash into riot, but so do high schools. The idea of armed police in the corridors of a public school is enough to make Thomas Arnold, who introduced the prefect system, moan in his grave.

Increasingly, it is seen that the school is unable to do what it did so powerfully and so effectively during the last three or four hundred years—and indeed what it is still doing in communist countries—educate for living, inculcate or strengthen social principles. The problem is that an educational system that was designed for an elite is breaking down in the attempt to educate the mass of industrial society, for which it was never designed. An elite is willing to be disciplined, to learn seemingly arcane subjects, such as Latin or medieval history or theology, because the rewards of success are obvious—high professional office, status in society, beckon at the end of the road. For the masses pouring into the public schools and universities all that beckons is a job in a factory or an office, with no guarantee, even, of social status. What is available for everyone distinguishes no one.

We are at the end of ten thousand years of history. We are in the middle of a revolution more profound than any man has experienced, and thus we are affected more deeply than we realize. Not only are age-old social institutions breaking down, but there is a greater problem. Men, women, and children are losing their ability to

identify with society; they no longer have clear social roles to fulfill, to aspire to, to feel guilty about if they fail in them. For the last ten thousand years fathers and mothers, husbands and wives, sons and daughters, in all societies have had defined social roles. And the crisis of identity we hear so much about arises not so much because the individual is lost, but because society no longer defines his function.

If mankind fails to find
new institutions
that enable him to cope
with industrialized
life, then there could be
a retreat, and
a very sharp retreat, from
scientific, technological,
urban civilization.

Consider the role of children. The power that parents hold over their children, and the need for the children to respect the authority and wisdom of age, have been almost universally accepted for the last ten thousand years. But now, with the weakening of the family, the respect and the subordination have both gone. Similarly the subordination of women; likewise the authority of men. Until recently, social roles were very strongly defined—of course, there were many who rebelled against them, many who failed to live up to them, and many more who found them constricting and disagreeable; but the majority of mankind accepted their social role, even if they rarely attained it. Women's liberation, the revolt of adolescence, and the decay of the patriarch are not signs of

the sudden fever that has gripped this generation; rather they are the product of a social revolution, of a need for radical readjustment, one such as man has had to make only once before in his history.

Whether man can live in so profoundly new a social complex is open to doubt. Understanding may help a little. Governments are always more conservative with regard to social change than society itself (witness the problem of divorce in Italy or legalized abortion here), but if governments realized that the social experimentation of our day is not due to the sickness of youth or the corruption and self-indulgence of this generation but has profound social causes, perhaps then they might help rather than hinder experiment.

But in the end men and women must themselves evolve new institutions and find new social roles that satisfy the innate needs of man and provide those necessary deep psychic protections and safeguards that we all require. The new roles will spring from man's great biological adaptability, if they spring at all. If mankind fails to find new institutions that enable him to cope with industrialized life, then there could be a retreat, and a very sharp retreat, from scientific, technological, urban civilization. New York or London might become the new Nineveh and Tyre, buried under vast ruins of their own detritus. And possibly, perhaps even probably, man will fail to cope at all: his aggressive and acquisitive drives, which are perhaps his deepest, may prevail. He may blow himself up or pollute himself off the face of the earth.

All possibilities are open, but man's capacity for social evolution, as recorded in his history, is exceptional, and the human psyche is resilient and tough. If and when a new world emerges from the discords of the old, it will probably be both varied and strange. There is one thing we can be sure of—it will be little like the world that we now live in.

ONLY YESTERDAY: A large, cohesive family, c. 1900

Our Crumbling Institutions

The institutions of civilized life—essentially unchanged since the agricultural revolution of ten thousand years ago—are showing signs of strain, if not collapse. Here, and on the following pages, HORIZON documents Professor Plumb's thesis.

IN OLDER TIMES: An early Christian family, c. 200

The Family

Until this century everybody knew that the family was "a natural association of kindred," to quote the *Encyclopedia Britannica* for 1911. It seemed to be not only a basic but an inevitable institution. To the farmer, the family was a work team; to the artisan, the family household was a workplace. It was everybody's most important school, often the only one. A man's relatives provided the bulk of his society. In our own time, however, the world of the family has shrunk drastically. It is no longer a work team, no longer the chief school for life, no longer a varied society in itself. Many now claim that the family is even unfit for child rearing and propose the young be reared by "communes" or by the state. For the first time in history the family seems to be losing its ultimate reason for being.

TODAY: The communal household of "Hog Farm"

IN OLDER TIMES: Ducal father tutors his son.

Education

Throughout the history of civilization the purpose of education has been beyond all dispute: to transmit to future adults the codified learning and culture that the adult world possessed. Whether a teacher stood before a village classroom or privately tutored the son of a lord, he represented that adult world and introduced the newcomers to it. Nobody doubted that he had much to teach and his students even more to learn. Students might rebel against a teacher, but not against the idea of being taught. Since the turn of the century, however, the entire rationale for education has been under attack. The teacher is not praised but criticized for merely transmitting adult mores to children. Adult codes appear irrelevant and restrictive, in a time of radical change a potential danger to the creativity and innocence of the young. The effects of this new belief—itself the product of revolutionary change—is obvious on all sides. Educators now speak of "de-schooling education" and allowing the young, as far as possible, to direct their own education. Teachers no longer claim authority because they no longer feel entitled to it. Students in rapidly increasing numbers now look on their schools as "prisons," and with police called in to keep order, a great many schools do indeed look like prisons.

TODAY: Policemen on guard in a New York City school

ONLY YESTERDAY: Pledging allegiance in 1899

IN OLDER TIMES: *Mourning rites in ancient Egypt*

Religion

Religion once loomed so large in man's life that civilization was inconceivable without it—even to a mocking Voltaire. Theology gave rich meaning to the universe; God's providence made sense of the vagaries of history and fortune. The local church was not only a place of worship, it was a civic center and a social forum that transformed its communicants into a community. If a man were an unbeliever, that, to his neighbors, was the most important fact about him. Yet today, the question of a man's faith hardly arises at all, for Western society has rapidly become the most secular civilization that has ever existed. In many countries, such as England, churchgoing itself is a vanishing practice. To many Americans as well, Sunday is no longer a day set aside, but merely a part of the weekend. Even the steady churchgoers are often "practical atheists," as a leading American divine has observed, so little does religion permeate their lives. Where people once heeded their clergy, today it is the churchmen who do the heeding, trying heroically to adapt their liturgies, their theologies, and even their politics to the passing currents of modern thought. Instead of encompassing life, organized religion has become one institution among many that are competing for modern man's divided attention.

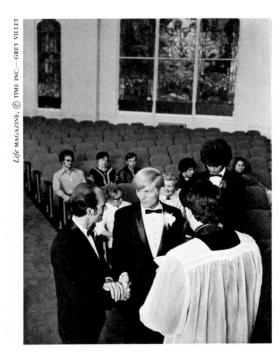

TODAY: *A minister blesses a homosexual marriage.*

ONLY YESTERDAY: *Church temperance group in Oregon, 1900*

IN OLDER TIMES: Roman soldiers arresting Christ

Law and Order

There is no surer sign of the new revolution than the worldwide breakdown of law and order, striking in volatile America but visible on every continent. What is crumbling is not respect for laws and lawmakers but the authority inherent in the law, its ability to enforce itself. It is this that ultimately lies behind the continually mounting crime rate, the rising levels of violence, and the fear-haunted streets of great cities. It lies behind the endemic petty lawlessness—littering parks within view of a litter basket, for example, or smoking in front of no-smoking signs, as if the law compelled defiance. It is seen, too, in the growing indifference of onlookers to such petty malefactions, as if the law were no business of mere private men.

It is surely epitomized in the vanishing authority of the police, for the policeman's authority derives solely from the law's authority. Not long ago, a city patrolman walked his beat as the confident embodiment of invincible law. Today, policemen often feel like enemy intruders patrolling a conquered terrain. No superficial causes can explain the waning of the law's authority, for it rests on deeper foundations than, for example, current modes of "permissive" child rearing, or the relative strictness of courts. Ultimately, it depends on a belief that men in pacific times are scarcely aware they hold: the belief that the law embodies profoundly legitimate purposes—maintaining the common institutions and the way of life that people find natural and legitimate. Under the pounding of the new revolution, however, the great institutions of society no longer feel natural and legitimate and law itself loses its legitimacy, begins to seem arbitrary and alien. When W. S. Gilbert observed in 1880 that "a policeman's lot is not a happy one," he prophesied better than he knew.

TODAY: A Chicago policeman bloodied by rioters

ONLY YESTERDAY: A New York policeman towing a drunk

ONLY YESTERDAY: Dorrance, Kansas, population 281 in 1910, compressed all the basic urban institutions into a compact settlement.

IN OLDER TIMES: The Acropolis dominates the Athenian polis.

The Urban Center

Until a few generations ago, humankind tended to live compactly, drawing together not only in cities but in the countryside as well. Whether it was the Athenian polis or a compact prairie village, social life was built around a local center. In our own time, however, people are deliberately moving apart. Communicating by telephone and automobile, they no longer need propinquity as a basic human bond. Human society is ceasing to be the society of the people nearby. A truly radical transformation, it implies a social order comprised of like-minded groups rooted in no special place, a moral order in which the injunction "love thy neighbor" may become as irrelevant as neighbors. Every highway that opens up new terrain for scattered living brings this new world order closer. How men will adapt to this new revolutionary world is beyond anyone's power of prediction.

TODAY: Swirling superhighway depopulates a district of Detroit

TARGET WITH FOUR FACES, 1955

Jasper Johns' Elusive Bull's-Eye

His paintings are enigmatic, hermetic, sometimes
didactic—not pop art, nor op art, nor anti-art. They may also be
the most influential works of the past decade

Jasper Johns's face, as a writer pointed out some years ago, resembles that of William S. Hart, the silent gunslinger of the silent Westerns. The narrow, crinkled eyes stare flatly, with an expression of ironic watchfulness, across the V of a gun sight or the end of a paintbrush at—in either case—a target. It is the mask of cool, of a dandy who shuts up *and* puts up.

What goes on behind that mask has provoked reams of critical speculation for more than a decade; it was fourteen years ago, to be exact, that the twenty-eight-year-old Johns had his first show at Leo Castelli's gallery in New York. Since he afterward became to the 1960's what Willem de Kooning was to the 1950's—the most influential American artist of the decade—it is difficult to remember with what an air of prodigy Jasper Johns burst upon New York. Trailing no discernible past behind him, he landed on point at center stage.

The biography is scanty: Born May 15, 1930, in Augusta, Georgia, the son of a farmer. Eighteen months of college at the University of South Carolina; one day at Hunter College in

Target with Four Faces, opposite, is the work that more than any other established Johns's reputation as a major new artist. The painted target here is surmounted by four apparently imprisoned plaster casts of half a female face. The effect for the viewer is mysterious and somehow sinister as well.

Jasper Johns in his studio

New York. Two years of Army service, mostly in Japan. Several years of drifting in Manhattan after he began, in 1952, to paint "seriously," supporting himself, but only just, through odd jobs, such as selling books and doing window displays for Tiffany's and other uptown stores with his friend Robert Rauschenberg. (Nearly all these early store-window Johnses have long since vanished. One, a papier-mâché clown with a red nose and button eyes, is now in a basement in Connecticut.)

"I had never heard of Jasper," Castelli recalls, "until I saw his *Green Target* in a show at the Jewish Museum in 1957. The name, the assonance I suppose—J. J.—stuck in my mind. And it was a very singular painting,

quite unlike anything I'd seen before. I meant to look him up, but I couldn't find out anything about him. Nobody else had ever heard of him, either. Then I was visiting Bob Rauschenberg one day, and he happened to mention a young painter who lived in the loft below, a friend named Jasper Johns. So I asked if I could visit. When the door opened, I was stupefied. You see, there they all were, just stacked around the wall . . . the flags, the targets, everything Jasper had done up to then. Possibly every dealer has one exquisite moment of discovery in his life, which seems to justify all the buying and selling. Vollard's was meeting Picasso. Certainly mine was Jasper."

Success is the most obvious characteristic of Johns's reputation, and it has turned out to be both a problem and an emblem: a problem, because it is self-contradicting; an emblem, because it anticipated and colored the consumer frenzy of New York art in the 1960's. Johns's first show was sold out, and he was all but unanimously elected the historical alternative to the broad, slashing, romantic art of the abstract expressionists; with him, and Rauschenberg, the decade was given its birth certificate. The Museum of Modern Art, a rather more powerful taste-making instrument then than now, bought three canvases from Johns's first show in 1958, an unheard-of gesture to an unknown painter; several other museums followed suit. If ever a reputation was launched by one swipe of the Establishment's hand, it was Johns's. This instant acceptance helped touch off the lunacies of pop ballyhoo: an avid public began looking for new Jaspers under every stone. To be seized as the paradigm of all-American success was a strange fate for so complex and reclusive an artist.

In 1959 Hilton Kramer (now an art critic for *The New York Times*) unburdened himself of the view that Johns's work was both "mock-naive" and corrupt: "His handpainted American flags, targets, numbers, and so on, are a kind of Grandma Moses version of Dada. But Dada sought to repudiate and criticize bourgeois values, whereas Johns . . . aims to please and confirm the decadent periphery of bourgeois taste." The years have not confirmed this irritable judgment. The "decadent periphery" was served not by Johns but by the hundreds of artists who, feeling the influence of his work, responded to it mechanically and blatantly, without a trace of the formidably intelligent maze of nuances, ironies, and sheer painterly skill with which Johns contrived to surround every image he produced.

It is grim enough to be the most influential artist in America, and New York's taxes on talent (to be paid at times, as by some abstract expressionists, in alcoholism, paranoia, and suicide) are dreadful. Johns's defense is withdrawal, a remarkable degree of public silence. Even his studio is an architectural irony: an unused bank on Houston Street in Manhattan, a bare room 100 feet square, with the old steel-sphinctered vaults below, where instead of bonds and safety-deposit boxes, Johns's paintings are stored. There can be no more succinct image of the interchangeability of imagination and capital that was the sustaining myth of the New York art market in the 1960's. The paintings Johns showed in 1958 have now increased in value forty or fifty fold. Johns's large painted version of Buckminster Fuller's Dymaxion world map (pages 24–25) was

MAP, 1961

purchased last year for some $200,000 —the highest price yet for a work by a living American artist, and probably the highest ever paid for a picture by a man of forty-one.

These statistics are not, perhaps, very interesting in themselves. Who remembers last month's million-dollar Van Gogh? But they cast an oblique light on the difficulties of Johns's position. American culture consumes stars. But Johns, in his public and private attitudes, tries to eschew the role of culture hero. The model here is Marcel Duchamp, who was Johns's friend. Much of Johns's work is a sustained

meditation on the lessons to be learned from the unique open-endedness of Duchamp's work. *According to What* (pages 28–29) is Johns's equivalent of Duchamp's *Tu m'* (1918), complete with a small canvas facing the picture surface and displaying the title on its back and a plaster cast of the leg of the art critic Barbara Rose. It swings from its half-chair at the top left-hand corner and casts a shadow, in the manner of the illusory shadows in Duchamp's earlier work.

The ethics of Duchamp's life were quite as important to Johns as the aesthetics, or procedures, of his work.

be inflated, like the stories about Picasso's virility. Johns takes a dead-pan pleasure in giving the most banal reasons for calling works of art into existence. His American flag, he once solemnly told a reporter from *Time,* came to him in a dream. Maybe so, or maybe Johns said it did to have a little fun with the idea of romantic inspiration (a flag is not *Kubla Khan,* after all).

Irony lies at the bottom of all of Johns's autodidactic reasoning. Indeed, it is partly through Johns's application of Duchamp's ironies that Duchamp replaced Picasso as the prototype of the "modern artist" in America —no longer a culture hero, but a man of distances and margins, concerned with the semantics of very precisely registered ambiguity. Cool replaces hot; the expressive personality gives way to the didactic one.

In the nineteenth century, Walter Pater wrote that art aspired to the condition of music—the perfect, internal harmony of parts. In the twentieth, Johns's proposition is that art aspires to the condition of silence. By definition no work of art can reach this state (art, inevitably, means *some* kind of discourse). But a void can surround an image; it can be enveloped by absences, as under a bell jar. So it is with the deliberate, one is tempted to write ostentatious, ordinariness of Johns's subject matter. There is not much to be thought, it seems, about a coat hanger, a flashlight, a set of numbers or letters, a brace of Ballantine ale cans, or—once you have dispensed with the patriotic associations, which are no concern of Johns's and have nothing to do with

In a characteristically brief epitaph on Duchamp in *Artforum* in 1968, Johns remarked that "The self attempts balance, descends. Perfume—the air was to stink of artists' egos. Himself, quickly torn to pieces. His tongue in his cheek." This is precisely in the spirit of Duchamp's statement that "The only refutation is indifference," and his elegantly matter-of-fact comment on fame (including, naturally, his own): "The idea of the great star comes directly from a sort of inflation of small anecdotes. It was the same in the past. It's not enough that two centuries later we have to look at certain people as

though they were in a museum; the entire thing is based on a made-up history."

There are plenty of anecdotes about Johns. Some of them are even true, like the story about the origin of *Painted Bronze,* the celebrated cast-bronze ale cans Johns made in 1960 (page 26). De Kooning, irritated by Leo Castelli, was heard to grumble that "that son of a bitch could sell a couple of beer cans." Johns overheard, thought it not a bad idea, and went back to the studio and made the work, which Castelli duly sold to the collector Robert Scull for $1,200. But such anecdotes cannot

23

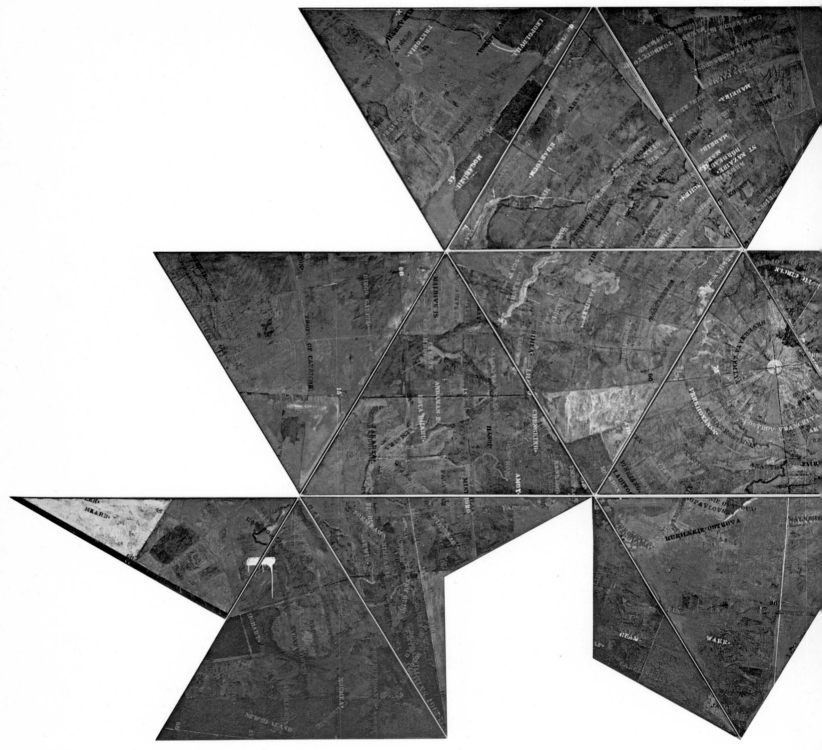

MAP, 1967–1971

his art—an American flag. Why, then, make them subjects of art?

Because, as Johns once put it, "Using the design of the American flag took care of a great deal for me because I didn't have to design it. So I went on to similar things like targets —things that the mind already knows. That gave me room to work on other levels."

One very important aspect of Johns's art is his preoccupation with what is sometimes called information overload. Everyone today endures a battering surplus of images that have no parallels in earlier centuries. J. Huizinga, in *The Waning of the Middle Ages,* points to the silence of medieval life: no cars or machinery, not much noise in the village beyond the wind, human voices, the clatter of carts, and the sound of animals. Against this muted background, cathedral music must indeed have seemed celestial. There was a hierarchy of sound, in contrast to our continuous level of it.

The same is true of what we see, not only in the ceaseless yabber of billboards and neon signs, but in the sphere of "fine" art. Never have so many paintings and sculptures been simultaneously available to such a culturally-obsessed audience. The clamor

24

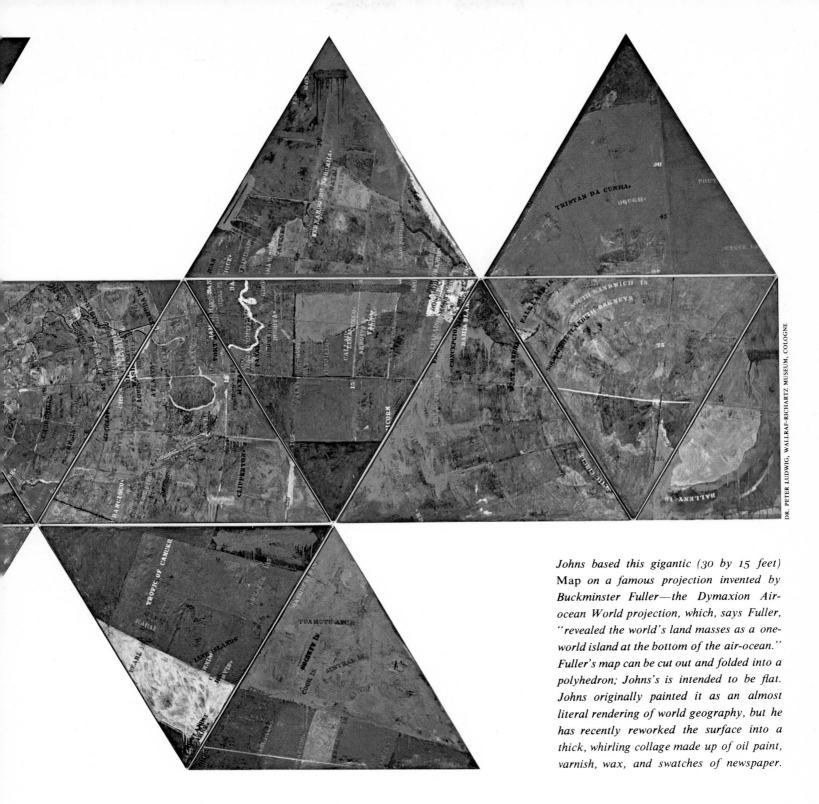

DR. PETER LUDWIG, WALLRAF-RICHARTZ MUSEUM, COLOGNE

*Johns based this gigantic (30 by 15 feet)
Map on a famous projection invented by
Buckminster Fuller—the Dymaxion Air-
ocean World projection, which, says Fuller,
"revealed the world's land masses as a one-
world island at the bottom of the air-ocean."
Fuller's map can be cut out and folded into a
polyhedron; Johns's is intended to be flat.
Johns originally painted it as an almost
literal rendering of world geography, but he
has recently reworked the surface into a
thick, whirling collage made up of oil paint,
varnish, wax, and swatches of newspaper.*

of historical styles becomes a kind of
Times Square. And what is the eye's
response to these callousing demands
on its time and focus? It retracts. Inattention is elevated to a survival technique. How does one rescue an image
—any image—from this flux and return it to credibility? As Johns has
said, "Already it's a great deal to see
anything *clearly,* for we don't see
anything clearly."

Thus the hermetic appearance of
Johns's early paintings and objects.
They address themselves to attention,
not description; inventory, not ar-
rangement. They have no narrative
content—not even the implied narrative of expressionist art, with its demonstration of the self through gesture.
The diabolic rigor with which Johns
keeps narrative out of his work can be
indicated by one example. *Target with*

Four Faces (page 20) involves a row of
four plaster casts of part of a girl's
face. Each is the same girl. But she became progressively more tired, and this
showed in the casts as a nearly imper-
ceptible slackening of her mouth. In
the painting Johns reversed casts three
and four, to avoid the look of accumu-
lating expression—of a "story."

Despite (or thanks to) such hidden
nuances, Johns's work can look be-

THREE FLAGS, 1958

PAINTED BRONZE, 1960

PAINTED BRONZE, 1960

wilderingly simple and bald, its declarations as flat as the enumerative descriptions in a catalogue novel by Butor or Robbe-Grillet. (This contributes to the common idea that his work has something to do with Neo-Dada, or the "revaluation" of ignoble subjects for their shock effect.) American flags are made of cloth. Can one imagine an American flag made of paint? And if there were an American flag made of paint, would it be a flag, or a painting, or both? And is a flag made of paint a painting *of* a flag, or does the fact of its being painted return it to the area of pure abstract design? The rendering of such a configuration in paint contrives in an extremely subtle way to change its use. For it will now attract more attention than is given to a flag. Perhaps a memory of my own will clarify the manner of this change. It has to do with shooting, and thus with targets.

As a boy in Australia one of my obsessions was target shooting with a .22 rifle. How a marksman sees a target defines its visual function, since a target has no use except to be shot at. And this way of seeing depends on selective inattention. Only the bull's-eye really matters. The outer rings are just for orientation. Looking at a target is an extreme case of hierarchical perception—10 for the bull, 7 for the inner-

most ring, and so on; and once you see a target aesthetically, as a unified design, its use is lost. The paradox is that a target is never scrutinized except in terms of an action that is not "seeing" —to wit, squeezing a trigger at the right moment. It is a sign, not an image. An image requires scrutiny and penetration; its "use" is the imaginative process of comprehending it, which happens more gradually. But one stares at a sign; it is unambiguous, clear and functional. Use and form are linked in a rigid way: use precedes form.

But what if use follows form? Can some change be made in the form of a target, and in the way of looking at it, that will cancel its use? That was the question Johns posed nearly twenty years ago in paintings like *Target with Four Faces* and *Target with Plaster Casts* (1955). His strategy was to switch the target's nature from sign back to image. You are forced to deal with the target's five rings—three greenish-blue ones, two yellow, centered on a rich red field—as painting and painting alone. This happens through the way they are painted: an even, sumptuous, almost edible skin of encaustic, so full of nuances and little incidents that the eye travels every inch of it with relish. No part is more "important," visually, than any other part, and the

idea of putting a bullet through it becomes absurd. What is there to aim at? Thus a sign, which can only be stared at, becomes a painterly image, which must be scanned.

But then one's attention moves to the boxes above, in which plaster casts of human parts are set. And there is still a degree of shock in realizing that Johns has pulled the reverse strategy: the human body, the image of art par excellence, is treated utterly schematically and rendered back into a system of signs, anonymous paint-dipped fossils that denote "face," "ear," "hand," or "penis." Johns's transformations of the organic and the inorganic have met and locked on a plane of logical paradox. You are left wondering what representation means. How can you represent a target or a flag when the act of painting it is exposed so logically as a process of changing its nature as sign into a new nature as image? How can you represent a number when a figure 7, whatever you do to it, remains a sign, stays itself? How did object and symbol ever get so close? One begins to see why Leo Steinberg, confronted for the first time with Johns's work, wrote in perplexity that "it is as if the subjective consciousness . . . had ceased to exist." And see, as well, what Johns meant when he said: "Generally, I am opposed to painting which is concerned

THE CRITIC SMILES, 1959

THE CRITIC SEES, 1961

The flag of his native land, like the map of it, is a motif that has preoccupied Johns, though both are divested of any political or patriotic significance in his canvases, one of which appears opposite at left. The pair of ale cans (opposite, center) is one of the works that inspired the pop-art movement, as is the bronze (opposite, right), which re-creates a coffee tin and paintbrushes. The objects at left are Johns's barbed offerings to his reviewers. The Critic Smiles is a prone toothbrush bedecked with four molars. The Critic Sees is a bas-relief of a pair of eyeglasses shielding toothy mouths behind the lenses.

with conceptions of simplicity. Everything looks very busy to me." Conceptual paradox is Jasper Johns's way of seeing clearly.

One could pursue this theme in his work, almost without limit. An obvious example is his play with colors and words *about* color: the letters R E D, for instance, stenciled in *blue* paint on an orange ground. Concept collides with sensation: the meanings cancel. The number paintings relate to this, and when Johns executed a lithograph of the number 7 with the Mona Lisa smiling from the sheltering curve of its downstroke, he formulated a brilliant metaphor for the primitive resentment of abstractness that lurks behind all numbers. (Probably this goes back to childhood. Children can comprehend numbers in their concrete form: four cauliflowers, eight apples. But the existence of numbers without things is frustrating.) The question "seven of *what?*" becomes the riddle of the Sphinx, neatly suited to the phony enigma of Leonardo's smile.

The peculiar absurdities of measurement and quantification are, indeed, one of Johns's favorite themes. One of his recurring objects is a wooden ruler, which crops up, in real or painted form, in various drawings and prints. (The prototype here, one may assume, is again Duchamp, whose *Three Standard*

Stoppages, 1913–24, were invented as an absurd, nonreferential unit of chance measurement, made by dropping a thread one meter long from a height of one meter onto a board and fixing it where it landed—a useless ruler.) Johns's ruler exists and is calibrated, and the only trouble is, as a point of strict logic, that once inside the painting it has nothing at all to measure. A picture has limits (its edges) but the turbulent space of paint inside is not measurable. Pictorial space is *felt* space, a matter of nuance, not inches, and so two modes of experience are again displayed as paradoxical, self-canceling.

Again, in his painted maps—of which the Buckminster Fuller world map is a provisional summing up—Johns deploys a whole battery of paradoxes. To begin with, the maps of the United States or the world are both recognizable *and* useless. You cannot navigate by them. In a sense, they are brilliant parodies of the abstract expressionist ideas that surrounded Johns's early development. American painting was much involved with the idea of epic landscapes, of getting into the center of a thoroughly romantic, cosmic image (as Pollock, Rothko, and Newman did). Johns takes this to the mock-logical irony of displaying the *whole* American landscape in map form, drenched and half-drowned in churn-

ing swathes of violently brushed pigment. In a blink, the hand smears its way from Iowa to Nebraska. It leaves out California, as one might suppress a tree in a landscape. One moment Johns is affirming that limits (here, geographic limits) can be measured; and the next, he is denying all its accuracy by the broad, splashy paint.

As Johns once admitted, this idea of the impossibility of limits was suggested to him by a passage in Leonardo's *Trattato della Pittura,* arguing that "the boundary of a body is neither a part of the enclosed body nor a part of the surrounding atmosphere." But Johns's approach has as much to do with Magritte as with Leonardo. His representations of maps relate to Magritte's famous representation of a pipe, with the words *"Ceci n'est pas une pipe"* beneath it. Of course it is not; it is a *picture.* So are the "maps."

Few painters have the icy detachment that would let them follow Johns all the way into his labyrinth of contradiction. Yet his influence on other artists (especially American artists) has been vast, not only as a moral presence on the scene, but as a stylistic one, too. Even though much of pop art is a vulgarization of Johns's use of banal, everyday signs and things, the ancestry is clear. But what is not so commonly acknowledged is Johns's influence, es-

ACCORDING TO WHAT, 1964

According to What, *reproduced above, is a sixteen-foot-long canvas incorporating various objects. One of Johns's major works, it has been praised as the "capstone of a decade." At top left is a plaster cast of a female leg attached to a chair-half, upside down. A small canvas with title (bottom left) unhooks to reveal a portrait of Marcel Duchamp, Johns's Dadaist mentor. Some of the big letters to the right are painted, some are aluminum objects that swing back and forth.*

pecially through his flags, on "literal" abstraction and minimal art. Much fuss was made of the "objectness" of the paintings of certain abstractionists in the 1960's, like Frank Stella. But in the mid-1950's Johns had already done his flags with no field behind them; the image, or sign, was the entire painting. At this point, he said, "it was clear that the painting was an object not a window," tightly structured and dense.

The swing from abstract expressionism to the new literalism of the sixties hinges on Johns's work. In this way, he begat two opposing tendencies, pop and minimal, that have fought it out, like Cain and Abel, in the galleries and art reviews ever since—under their sire's neutral and detached gaze. This gives an additional edge to some of Johns's more openly polemic objects, like his famous *The Critic Sees* (1961):

a pair of Sculpmetal spectacles, with mouths, not eyes, behind them. For, by any standard, Johns is not only the critic's artist—having attracted more words of explication, praise, and rebuke than anyone of his generation— but the critic's critic, too. In his work he has contrived to expose and clarify most of the interesting issues related to art in the past decade, and to do it better than words normally can.

At the same time, his work exists with exemplary purity *as painting,* creating fresh structures of visual experience. "Everything in nature," Jasper Johns has remarked, "has limitless possibilities. In my work, there is some attempt to distinguish the possibilities." There is an echo in that sentence. Leonardo, with whom Johns is obsessed—it is a curious coincidence that his career as a painter started in 1952, the five-

hundredth anniversary of Leonardo's birth—expressed the same amazement at the world's polymorphism: *"Il mondo e pieno d'infinite ragioni che non furono mai in isperienza"*—"The world is full of an infinity of causes which were never set forth in experience."

Few writers are better equipped to talk about modern artists than Robert Hughes, who is the art critic for Time.

ALL ILLUSTRATIONS COURTESY OF THOMAS J. WATSON LIBRARY, METROPOLITAN MUSEUM OF ART, NEW YORK; ALL DRAWINGS BY GEORGES LEPAPE; THIS PAGE: *Gazette du Bon Ton*, 1912; OPPOSITE: COLLECTION OF RENE DAZY, PARIS

"With splendid eyes . . . and a cruel mouth like a carp's," this "glittering, slouching" young thing epitomizes the new ideal created and vigorously marketed by Paul Poiret. Her high-waisted dress, a 1912 sensation, includes a Poiret trademark: the lampshade tunic. Like the other Poiret creations on the following pages, this one was drawn by the gifted artist Georges Lepape.

The Man Who Banned The Corset

A decree from fashion's dictator Paul Poiret
delivered women from one snare,
but he would set new ones: the hobble skirt
and the calorie count

Surely as much as any man does, Paul Poiret, couturier, merits a niche in the women's liberation hall of fame. For he was the fashion revolutionary who, at the beginning of this century, freed women from the corset. "I declared war on the corset," Poiret said. "Like all great revolutions, mine was carried out in the name of Liberty, to give free play to the stomach, which could dilate without restriction."

Others had been trying to achieve this since the 1850's, but with little success. There had been, for instance, the dress-reform ladies, with Amelia Jenks Bloomer in the forefront, and the British Aesthetes, with their anti-whalebone doctrine and unfettered Grecian draperies. But Poiret had an advantage over his predecessors. In addition to the usual attributes of the dedicated revolutionary— a sense of mission and a full measure of ego—he possessed a remarkable aptitude for drawing attention to himself. This instinct for showmanship carried him to power in 1907, to reign as king of fashion for nearly a quarter of a century. During this time he left his imprint on dress, art, and decoration. Traces of his influence linger with

Poiret was a dandy who loved women and elegant cars.

us still, in relaxed, unconstructed clothing that reveals the figure, and in the revival of the Art-Deco style that he to a large extent created.

"Imperious and Venetian" in his own eyes, and looking to Jean Cocteau like "some sort of huge chestnut," Poiret presented an impressive appearance. Once he took over the world of fashion, he had no trouble in exerting a

one-man rule, with a range of activities that extended from the designing of theatre costumes to the breaking down of social barriers. He expanded haute couture by branching out into related fields such as fabric design and interior decoration, and into the production of perfume and accessories, thus paving the way for wide-ranging enterprises of the mode like those of Dior, Cardin, and Yves Saint Laurent today.

"He was one of the very great creators in the history of fashion," a French authority has written. "A dress by Poiret is recognizable at a glance, like a painting by Renoir."

Poiret launched "the age of gold lamé." In his heyday, on the eve of World War I, he put women—uncorseted women— into pearl chin-straps and sent them off to the races wearing satin turbans spiked with tufts of aigrette feathers, trouser-skirts, and gold-embroidered Chinese cloaks. It was all part of the thrilling new vogue for Neo-Orientalism, a movement sparked by Poiret and Diaghilev's Ballet Russe, a vogue that made the generous Edwardian S-shaped figure, with its layers of lacy, complicated underclothes, seem hopelessly *démodé*.

By PHYLLIS FELDKAMP

ALL: *Les Choses de Paul Poiret, 1911*

In 1911 one wore harem pants chez soi . . .

"Yes," wrote Poiret, "I advocated the fall of the corset. I liberated the bust. When I declared war on the corset, women's bodies were divided into two distinct masses and the upper lobe appeared to be pulling the whole derrière section along behind it, like a trailer."

The elegant corset, of heavy colored silk or satin trimmed with real lace and ribbon bows, consisted of ten to fifteen curved pieces, not counting the gussets, and was traversed from end to end by dozens of whalebones and steel stays. Under it, a lady wore a garment called a chemise, which looked like a long nightshirt; over it, she—or more likely, her maid—hoisted voluminous linen pantaloons. On top of all this went a corset cover, a decorous bodice that concealed her stays. Finally, before being buttonhooked into her dress, she got into one, two, or even three elaborate petticoats coyly known as "frillies." The deployment of frillies was a tactic every flirt had to master. "As I knew my frillies were all right," said Elinor Glyn's Elizabeth in *The Visits of Elizabeth,* "I hammocked—and it was lovely."

The height of the corset-and-frillies era was *la belle époque,* when "Frou-Frou" was having her moment at

Maxim's and when the real standard-bearers of the mode were the flamboyant demimondaines. These imposing creatures held up their vast and snowy bosoms with stiff, boardlike constructions that ironed out their plump stomachs and pinched their waists in sharply at the back.

Then, overnight, they disappeared. The images of their *grandes toilettes* and jeweled dog-collars vanished from the gilded frames of the theatre loges in what Cocteau has described as a sort of lap-dissolve: the hard lines of the great cocottes gave way to the fluid ones of the new ideal—the glittering, slouching Poiret girl in her flowing, high-waisted dress, with splendid eyes, a headache band, curly hair dressed like a poodle's, and a cruel mouth like a carp's. Girls become conscious of their bodies and of calorie counting. Extra fat could be covered up by petticoats and leg-of-mutton sleeves, but not by the slinky Poiret line.

Years ahead of Rudi Gernreich's topless clothes and Saint Laurent's see-throughs, Poiret shocked the conventionally-minded by recommending that his customers wear nothing at all under the transparent tops of his dresses, advice that was eagerly taken by a fearless but not always shapely vanguard. The bra, as we know it, had yet to be invented. Breasts à la Poiret were breasts as nature made them, without benefit of modern sports and exercises, lifted only by the grosgrain cummerbunds he sewed inside the rib cages of his Empire-style dresses.

Pre-Poiret, overendowed ladies had worn "correctors," or "flatteners," while the underendowed had filled themselves out with the contemporary version of falsies—flounced linen "amplifiers." Such rectifiers were regarded as an improvement over both the cotton wadding that was stuffed into the tops of nineteenth-century corsets and the padded "bust improvers" introduced in the 1880's by Charles Frederick Worth, who fought a long, lonely battle against the cumbersome crinoline.

When Poiret started out in high fashion, Paris was its undisputed center. The son of a draper who had a small store on the rue des Deux-Ecus in Paris, he showed his talent for dressmaking early. He never played much with other children; his sisters used some of their savings to buy him a miniature mannequin, which he clothed with scraps of silk from the shop of the umbrella maker to whom he was apprenticed. Another of his talents—the prodigality that was to lead to his downfall—exhibited itself early, too. With the first sizable bonus he received when he was working for the couturier Jacques Doucet, Poiret went out and bought himself expensive opal cufflinks.

At that time, a handful of Paris designers, led by the powerful, conservative house of Worth, dictated the styles, which were then worn by a few choice ladies. Sooner or later, the rest of the world followed their example. The Maison Worth, which had been pre-eminent since Charles Frederick had made his international reputation under Napoleon III as couturier to the empress Eugénie, was under the direction of his sons, Monsieur Jean and Monsieur Gaston.

Their clients included almost every royal family in Europe. While Worth dressed the aristocracy, the rival house

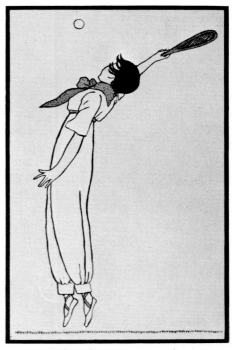

. . . *and outdoors, too,* pour le sport

of Doucet produced flashier clothes for the noted actresses and demimondaines. The brothers Worth knew of Poiret as Doucet's up-and-coming assistant designer, who, besides creating costumes for Réjane and Sarah Bernhardt, had turned out as his first model a deceptively plain little wrap of red coachman's cloth that customers had ordered four hundred times. They summoned him into their presence.

As Monsieur Gaston explained to Poiret, his aristocratic clientele no longer dressed exclusively in gowns of state: "Princesses sometimes take buses. They even walk on foot in the street. My brother Jean has always refused to make a certain type of dress, a simple and practical dress. And yet we are being asked for them. We are in the situation of a great restaurant which is only accustomed to serving truffles. But we are obliged to create a department of fried potatoes."

Hired as the *pommes frites* specialist, Poiret was appalled to discover *"les exubérances de Père Worth"* still influencing the house. Charles Frederick's tastes had run to dresses festooned with telegraph wires on which flocks of swallows perched, or to embroideries of large snails. Monsieur Jean, for his part, was upset by Poiret's novel interpretations of elegance. "You call that a dress?" he would ask, looking at one of Poiret's tailored models. "I call it a piece of trash."

Nor were all the princesses who dressed at Worth ready for Poiret's versions of the simple and practical. *"Quelle horreur!"* gasped a Russian princess when she had a look at an austere black kimono coat by Poiret.

In 1904, deciding the time had come to strike out on his own, Poiret set himself up, with his mother's backing, in a modest boutique on the rue Auber. There and at the *hôtel particulier* on the rue Pasquier where he installed himself two years later, he put on fashion *défilés,* the first shows of their kind, for the Parisian society women who, by invitation only, packed the house each afternoon from five to seven.

According to one observer of the daily parade, mannequins undulated "in lighting knowingly lowered, with steps in voluptuous rhythm and in hieratic poses, women turbanned in red, in blue, or in multicolored madras, measuring their slow tread in girdles of silken velvet." A talented young photographer named Edward Steichen took soft-focus pictures of them. Their stance developed into the round-shouldered, hipbones-forward gait that lasted through the twenties and that Cocteau called "the praying mantis walk."

Poiret set the traditionalists back on their heels with his startling use of color.

Scheherazade turban with aigrette feathers

"I hunted down the morbid mauves, the neurasthenic pastels," he said, "and into this sheepcote I threw a few rough wolves—the reds, the greens, the violets and royal blues that made the pale and neutral colors sing." He chucked the corset, but he set a new snare. "I shackled the legs. I remember the tears, the cries, the grindings of the teeth this decree brought forth in the world of the mode. Women complained that they could not walk anymore, they could not get into a carriage. And yet everybody wore the narrow skirt."

With the hobble skirt came other Poiret trademarks: the soft, clinging bodice, the loose harem pants, the classical Grecian draperies, and the lampshade tunic. The draperies suited his friend Isadora Duncan, whom he

introduced to Paris at one of his lavish parties, and were also appropriated by England's answer to Isadora, Maude Allen, who popularized an early see-through style sometimes referred to as "Le Nude." But impropriety in dress could not make much headway in England, at least not in the opinion of fashion scholar C. Willett Cunnington. "When the French dress designers, with their depraved minds, tried to bifurcate the hobble skirt into Turkish trousers," he has written, "the English conscience rebelled." The French took a practical view. Hobble skirts slit to the knee or divided into harem pants were, they found, the solution to what to wear while doing the tango, the new dance craze.

The mysterious East had become all the rage. Poiret, who had never been closer to Asia than a course in Tamil at the University of Paris, was largely responsible for the uncertain mélange of Oriental motifs that characterized the fashions of the day. He shifted his inspirational sights from classical Greece to Persia to ancient Egypt to China and back again before the public could catch up with him.

The intellectually inclined were then reading Dr. Joseph Charles-Victor Mardrus's highly colored translation into French of *The Arabian Nights*. The popular reading was Elinor Glyn's novel *Three Weeks*. In it, the heroine, a passionate Balkan queen, spends the major part of her time lolling about on a tiger-skin rug; and in many a fashionable house the "Turkish Corner," a nook *Vogue* had touted at the turn of the century as "a dream of comfort and elegance," was already an established feature. So was smoking hashish—or pretending to. Hookahs and foot-long cigarette holders were the chic accessories when one leaned languorously back on stacks of pillows under one of the new electric lamps.

In 1908 Poiret took over a dilapidated eighteenth-century *hôtel particulier* with a large courtyard in which chickens were running about loose and announced that he was going to do it over in high seraglio style. The news set off a boom in Oriental decorations. Dealers at the Flea Market experienced a run on such items as peacock feathers and bits of lacquer, as debutantes with hazy notions about the East went hunting for Oriental bric-a-brac. "Do you have any Coromandel?" one young thing asked another. "I should say I do," the second replied. "Why, I even have some signed by him."

To help him decorate his new house, Poiret had the collaboration of Suë et Mare. Louis Suë was an architect, furniture designer, and decorator who, with André Mare, organized an atelier that eventually employed artists like La Fresnaye, Dunoyer de Segonzac, Maillol, and Despiau. Suë et Mare's furnishings for Poiret—lush metallic curtains, lacquered panels, and thick Persian rugs—inspired the duchesses and actresses Poiret dressed to redo their own interiors, with a wealth of wrought-iron grills, Lalique glass, and lampshades with dangling silk fringe.

To the distress of their husbands, they also heaped floors and sofas with masses of cushions. For years to come, men on both sides of the Channel—and the ocean, for that matter—would grumble about pillows. "I say, Monica," complains a man sprawled across the floor in a 1924 *Punch* cartoon, "do let's leave Chelsea and sit on chairs again."

The part of pasha that Poiret so enjoyed playing was a matter of typecasting. Plump, gregarious, and epicurean, Poiret became an inveterate womanizer from the moment his early employer, Doucet, suggested he take a *petite amie* to be a truly worldly Parisian. He went on to a series of liaisons with willing actresses who seldom, in consequence, had to pay for their clothes. With mannequins and other young women on his staff, however, his manner was less sultanic than schoolmasterish, although he did once advise a virtuous *première* in his workroom that she would better understand the sensual charm of his creations if she had a lover.

Poiret's finest hour came one night in May, 1911, when in his Faubourg Saint Honoré house he gave a historic fete, the ball of *La Mille et Deuxième Nuit*. Raoul Dufy concocted the invitations. The guests were asked to come in Persian garb, and those who arrived in ordinary dinner or evening clothes were dispatched upstairs to choose costumes from a wardrobe their host had provided. Poiret's artist friends relied on ingenuity. Guy-Pierre Fauconnet, who was out of funds, wrapped himself in several lengths of white sheeting, with a result so effectively Middle Eastern that many declared him the best-dressed man in the crowd. Steichen got by the door check in an African burnoose.

Snobs like the elderly lady in pink satin harem pants, accompanied by a gentleman clad as a janissary, claimed to have come merely out of curiosity. Spotting nobility among the throng, she observed that society must be turning topsy-turvy, for "*grandes dames* now accept invitations from their tradespeople."

Les Choses de Paul Poiret, 1911; OPPOSITE, TOP RIGHT: SAME

Enter shy miss, in Empire-style gown

A torch-bearing flunky naked to the waist and draped below in cloth of gold escorted guests across eight yards of carpet that Dunoyer de Segonzac had painted especially for the party, through a sanded, canopied forecourt filled with spouting fountains to a blue and gold portal leading to a series of *divertissements*. One of these was the sultan's favorite, Mme Poiret, in gold lamé, imprisoned in a huge gilded cage filled with rare birds and a covey of dancing girls who hummed Persian airs as they fed their goldfish, admired themselves in mirrors, and ate ices.

Poiret himself, rigged out as a caliph in a caftan of silver brocade with a gigantic cabochon emerald at his waist and a large turban on his head, received the salaams of his guests from a throne atop a tier of steps covered with writhing nymphs. The nymphs were clothed mostly in beads and wore frightened expressions. Glowering through spectacles perched on his false nose, the couturier abandoned himself to his role and as the evening progressed, flicked his tiny ivory whip at passing houris.

Among the night's other entertainments were a python tamer with diamond-encrusted teeth; a sook featuring a fortuneteller, a potter's wheel, and Turkish delight; and a slave-girl dealer. Tales from *The Arabian Nights* were declaimed by the great tragedian Edouard de Max, his eyes ringed with kohl and wearing a fortune in pearls.

A South American tourist who stumbled over several of the nude odalisques that Poiret had arranged here and there in the garden, under gauze, responded by quoting suitably from Omar Khayyám. As dinner was served, forty blackamoors burned myrrh and incense. (Poiret had not yet concocted the pungent perfume he was later to market under the name "Night of China.")

The Arabic dances outdoors were illuminated by swarms of phosphorescent insects that Poiret had positioned in the trees. When the time came, after midnight, to ignite the fireworks, the sparks nearly finished off the Boukhara carpets on the lawn. The insects released with the *feu d'artifice* did not upset the peacock or the flamingos, which were indoors, but they did unnerve the monkeys and the parakeets fastened to the branches; many of them got loose and were found the next morning shrieking up and down the Champs Elysées.

Poiret gave other parties after that, but none ever equaled *La Mille et Deuxième Nuit*—not even the one he threw at Butard, the hunting lodge built by Jacques Ange Gabriel for Louis XV, although nine hundred bottles' worth of champagne flowed and Poiret received his three hundred guests done up as Jupiter, his hair and beard painted gold. But he never stopped trying. He bought a yacht and took dozens of friends on leisurely Mediterranean cruises. When he summered at Deauville, he rented a whole string of houses for friends, to be sure of having congenial neighbors.

His black Hispano-Suiza leading the way, Poiret toured Europe with his mannequins, who wore glazed linen hats marked with the monogram "PP." He started a decorating firm and "introduced" the sunken bathtub. He joined forces with Dufy to experiment with dyes while Dufy created a group of uncommon silk fabrics that have since become collectors' items.

One of his most influential enterprises, the Ecole Martine, a school he started for the daughters of factory workers, led to the Art-Deco style. The girls were taken out to look at nature and then asked to paint the birds, trees, and flowers they had seen. Their fresh, naive pictures were used as basic designs for the production of pottery, fabrics, and wallpaper.

World War I, in which Poiret's army duties included the creation of new uniforms, altered his fortunes. When peace came, he opened a new salon on the Rond Point des Champs-Elysées, but he ran into financial difficulties. His nightclub, *L'Oasis,* had but a relatively brief success. The money and effort he put into decorating and furnishing three houseboats on the Seine for the 1925 Exposition des Arts-Décoratifs were largely wasted because the exposition opened at a time of year when all the rich had left for their country places.

As Poiret's power declined, in the 1920's, he went on the lecture circuit in the United States, where he was billed as the "King of Fashion." He was flattered by the title, he told his audiences, but he did not want to be a despot or a dictator. "I am not your master," he said. "I am your slave, hoping to divine your secret desires. Women are perpetually falling in love with change, perishing with thirst for something new."

But his ability to divine these secret desires waned. By the mid-1930's his prodigality and disdain for the practical side of business had done him in; he left his family and retired to the south of France to paint. During World War II he was once observed sauntering along the jetty of a Mediterranean port in an admiral's hat and a suit he had cut from a terry-cloth bathrobe, a pair of scissors in his pocket.

When his family located him Poiret had lost seventy pounds and was suffering from Parkinson's disease. He went back to Paris, and died there of a heart attack in 1944.

During the days of his fashion revolution Poiret bore in mind that "there has never been a truly new fashion

Eastern motif: slave, parrot, slinky dress

which has not caused, at the outset, as Beaumarchais said, a general hue and cry, a universal chorus of hatred and proscription." But when Gabrielle Chanel took over the clothing of the revolutionary figure early in the jazz age, Poiret behaved like a middle-aged conservative who does not want to be reminded of his own youthful indiscretions. "Women were beautiful and architectural like ships' figureheads," he said. "Now they look like undernourished telegraph operators."

Once, however, in 1927, he recovered his prophetic sense. In "Will Skirts Disappear?" an article for *The Forum,* he looked ahead toward our time, making an eerily accurate prediction of a synthetic, plastic future. He saw hats of spun glass, pants of natural palm fiber, fichus of incandescent vegetable silk. The Rodiers of the day would be supplied by their chemist with cellulosahs in acidulated tints, sulfurated glucosinahs that shimmered. Women would wear tunics of scintillating silver, apple-green gandourahs, trousers of paprika satin, pale blue shocks of hair. . . .

He was right.

The fashion editor of the Philadelphia Bulletin, *Phyllis Feldkamp spent twelve years in Paris free-lancing. Her article on Paul Poiret will appear in a book she has written with her husband Fred on the pleasures of life in France. Harper's Magazine Press will publish it this fall as* The Good Life—or What's Left of It.

Gazette du Bon Ton, 1914

Poiret's hobble skirt: "I shackled the legs."

THE
RAMAYANA

Throughout Southeast Asia hundreds of millions of people, a fifth of humanity, still listen, enthralled, to an ancient story: an exiled prince's long, thrilling struggle to rescue his beautiful wife from her demon abductor

By SANTHA RAMA RAU

It was, exotically enough, in Luang Prabang, the royal capital of Laos, that I first realized that there was a different —indeed, to my conventional Indian eyes, an altogether revolutionary—interpretation of the great Hindu epic the *Ramayana*. Like most Indians, I had been brought up on the immortal story of the *Ramayana,* on its poetry, its mythology, but most of all, on its moral substance, on the splendid, unquestioned prototypes it set in its hero and heroine, Rama and Sita, of the perfect human beings.

Until then, I had never imagined that they could be less than ideal. So perfect was Rama in his piety, righteousness, strength, obedience, and respect of wis-

dom that he rated the recognition of the gods and was eventually elevated to their number. Even so unorthodox a Hindu as Mahatma Gandhi died from his assassin's bullets with the hallowed name "Ram, Ram" as his last words, simultaneously forgiving his murderer and invoking the blessing of the deity.

Sita, Rama's dutiful, loving, and incorruptible wife, dedicated solely to the happiness and welfare of her husband, has become in India the ideal of Hindu womanhood. A mother's last words to her daughter after her marriage are traditionally, "Be as Sita, be as Savitri" (another devoted wife from the monumental expanse of Hindu mythology). The *Ramayana* holds a special place

in Indian hearts. Primarily, I suppose, it is because the basic story is so simple and so dramatic that, unlike the complexities of action and the huge cast of disparate and intricately related characters in the *Mahabharata,* the larger of the two great Hindu epics, the *Ramayana* is immediately and grippingly accessible to any age group. I can remember as a very young child how my grandmother would stretch out on the *thakhat,* a wooden platform covered with white hand-woven cotton and bolsters, set out in the courtyard of her house. It would be just at the time when the first cool of the brief evenings of the Hot Weather brought a light breeze through the orchards and gar-

At a festival of the Ramayana *in Prambanan, Java, a troupe of dancers re-creates the climax of the epic: Rama (danced by a woman) brandishes a sword, as his warriors circle the enemy, Ravana, who has raised one of them aloft. The carving below, of Rama and Sita, is from the temple in the background.*

Ravana, though Rama's opponent, appears in some versions of the epic as a tragic hero. Each of the peoples of Southeast Asia has made the Ramayana *distinctly its own, and in this twelfth-century bas-relief at Angkor, in Cambodia, the demon king wears the features of a native Khmer.*

dens, and she would call the children of the family to her and would read to us.

As soon as we saw her large, worn copy of the *Ramayana,* we prepared ourselves for a treat. She would open the book at random and begin reading from the start of whichever adventure she happened on, explaining the difficult passages, sometimes asking what we would have done or what the truly virtuous person would have done in this or that predicament, subtly instilling in us the tenets of proper moral behavior. At last, when the kerosene lanterns had been lit and the silly moths had started bumping blindly into them, we would be sent off to bed, our heads filled with gods and demons and heroic deeds.

In essence, the *Ramayana* tells of the young Prince Rama of Ayodhya, whose father, in his declining years, impressed by the just, noble, and kingly qualities of his eldest son, decides to abdicate his throne and announce the coronation of Rama. Instead, through malice and trickery, he is compelled to send his son into exile for fourteen years, while a younger brother, Bharata, is crowned in Rama's place.

Rama, his loyal brother, Lakshmana, and his devoted wife, Sita, set out, followed by the lamentations of their subjects and the brokenhearted blessings of the dying king, to follow this destiny without bitterness, with good grace, and even with joyful expectations of learning much from the religious hermits and sages who have made their own rigorously austere enclaves of prayer and meditation in the forests. For ten years they wander, meeting wise men, having adventures and finding themselves in conflict with evil spirits and demons, living on whatever food they can find or on game that Rama and Lakshmana, both expert archers, manage to kill.

Eventually, news of Sita and the two brothers in their forest exile reaches Ravana, the ten-headed Demon King of Lanka—or, as we know it, Ceylon. Ravana's sister, a fierce giantess, has seen Rama on one of her mischief-making journeys, and she tries to seduce him. Meeting no success, she then tries her wiles on Lakshmana, and is spurned again. Convinced that both brothers are in love with Sita, she attempts, in a fit of jealousy, to swallow her. Lakshmana springs to Sita's defense and so mutilates the giantess that she returns to her brother with her

nose, ears, and breasts severed, demanding revenge.

Ravana is not particularly interested in revenge, and it is only when he hears a description of Sita's unparalleled beauty, grace, and elegance that he determines to capture this pearl among women for himself. He orders one of his demon subjects to take the form of a golden deer of incredible charm, with bewitching liquid eyes, jewel-encrusted horns, and tiny hooves of alabaster. Sita sees this enchanting creature and begs Rama to catch it for her.

Unable to resist her pleading, he sets out after the deer, instructing Lakshmana to guard Sita every moment that he is gone. But no sooner has the little deer led Rama out of sight of their forest dwelling than Lakshmana and Sita hear the unmistakable voice of Rama calling for help in increasingly anguished tones. At first Lakshmana refuses to leave Sita, but the demon's imitation of Rama's voice is too realistic and heart-rending for Sita to bear, and at last she presuades Lakshmana to go to his brother's aid.

This is, of course, the moment arranged by Ravana to fly up from his island stronghold on his miraculous winged chariot, swifter than the wind, and carry Sita off to his palace. Helpless and overpowered, she can only plead for mercy, weep at her credulousness, beg the rivers and forests to tell Rama *somehow* of her plight, and more practically, drop her few pieces of jewelry along the way as she and Ravana speed back to Lanka. Only once during the journey does any creature try to stop the all-powerful Ravana. The good king of the vultures attacks the flying chariot, but falls, fatally wounded, to earth.

In his fabulous city, built mostly of gold and protected by wide moats and impregnable stone and metal walls, Ravana tries all the blandishments he can think of to soften Sita's feelings toward him—jewelry, fine clothes, rare flowers to adorn her, handmaidens to serve her, pleasure gardens and tame animals to amuse her, musicians and dancers to perform for her. But she is adamant. Her marriage vows and her love for Rama are unassailable. She will accept none of Ravana's gifts; she would rather go barefoot and wear the faded remnants of her own sari, without ornaments, her hair hanging loose and untended, than be seduced by Lanka's king or the luxury he offers.

Meanwhile, Rama and Lakshmana, realizing that they have been deceived by a demon's stratagem, set out on a long journey across India looking for clues to Sita's whereabouts. Eventually, after countless adventures and feats of courage and endurance, they find the dying king of the vultures, who lives only long enough to tell the brothers of Sita's fate and to identify her captor.

Now comes the almost equally daunting problem of how to rescue her. Again the brothers overcome a series of hazards and obstacles, fights and betrayals, until they enlist as their allies Sugriva, the king of the monkeys, and his wise old general, Hanuman. Monkey scouts are sent out all over the country, but it is Hanuman who actually penetrates Ravana's fortress, finds Sita, and gives her Rama's signet ring to prove his good faith and to assure her that rescue is on the way.

Hanuman, being, after all, a monkey, can't resist taunting Ravana by larking about in the palace gardens pulling up plants. Finally he insults the king by raising himself up on his coiled tail to seat himself at a higher level than royalty. Ravana would like to kill him, but remembering that the code of battle forbids the execution of an emissary from the opposing side, he spares his life. To avenge the insult, however, he has Hanuman's tail wrapped in oily rags and set on fire—a most discourteous thing to do to a monkey. Hanuman, irrepressible still, uses his flaming tail to set fire to whatever is combustible in the fortress city, then flies back to the brothers to recount his deeds.

Now Sugriva's great army of monkeys, led by Hanuman, mobilizes to build a causeway with colossal boulders

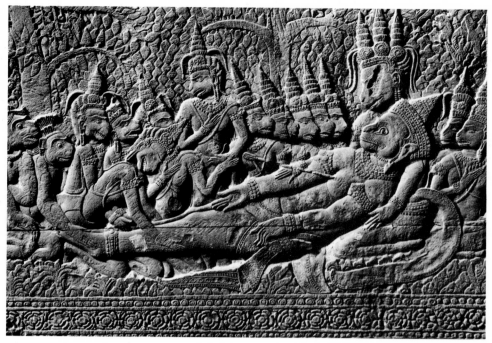

The adventures of the Ramayana's *numerous monkey heroes figure prominently in sculpture throughout Southeast Asia. In the one above, also at Angkor, a monkey king who has made the mistake of battling an ally of Rama lies dying in his wife's arms, the victim of Rama's arrow.*

from the Himalayas, and massive uprooted trees, across the strait that separates India from Ceylon. Remnants of the causeway, or at least of *a* causeway, can still be seen. And it is still called Rama's Bridge.

Once the brothers and the monkey army have reached Lanka, helped by the military intelligence provided by a defecting brother of Ravana's about fortifications, defenses, and the deployment of troops, there begins the famous, the fabulous, the inexhaustibly thrilling ten-day battle, filled with individual acts of courage, heroic deeds, hand-to-hand combat, and the massacre of whole armies. One after another, the great generals and warriors of Ravana's forces bring out their troops to defeat the invaders. But in the end Rama is triumphant. He alone, after the mightiest of confrontations, kills the Demon King of Lanka and frees Sita.

A happy ending? Not quite yet.

The story has a curious epilogue, and perhaps it is this that gives the Laotian view of the epic such an unusual twist. When Sita at last comes out of captivity to greet her husband in an ecstatic reunion, she is met instead with chilly formality. It is one thing, Rama seems to claim, that she has sworn to her fi-

delity during her years in Ravana's palace, but quite another that she might be telling the truth. Who, after all, can testify to the virtue of a woman?

Sita, in despair, agrees to undergo an ordeal by fire to clear herself of suspicion, and Rama (outrageously ungallantly, in the Laotian opinion) allows her to perform this horrifying act of exculpation. The fire god Agni, and even the sky itself, stunned by Sita's bravery, proclaim her innocence, and only then does Rama accept her back, saying that *he* has never doubted her word. He only wanted public proof. The Laotians put considerable ironic emphasis on this blatant disingenuousness.

Even with some reservations, a happy ending *now?* Not quite yet.

There is a further episide—added, according to some scholars, many years after the original text—that gives more material for the Laotian view. When Rama and Sita finally return to Ayodhya, Bharata humbly restores the throne to its rightful heir, removing from it Rama's sandals, which he has left there for fourteen years as a symbol to remind the people of their true king. After the coronation, the festivities, and the beginning of a reign of such unprecedented peace and prosperity that even now a *"Ramarajya"* (rule of Rama) has come to mean a utopian state, Rama is still uncertain of Sita's purity.

One day he sees a washerman beating his wife. He learns that the washerman's neighbors think his wife has been unfaithful to him, so he has decided he must punish her publicly. This ridiculous incident, instead of arousing Rama's sympathy for the poor woman, so impresses him that he fears for Sita's, but primarily his own, reputation. He hears that there have been murmurs of doubt among some of his subjects. How, when her ordeal by fire had taken place hundreds of miles away, are they to be convinced?

In short, he cannot allow his reputation as the perfect, pious, and just monarch to be impaired by the suspicion that he has taken back an adulterous woman. His Public Image is at stake. What is more, Sita is pregnant. A ten-headed demon like Ravana as an heir? No, the risk is too great.

He banishes Sita to the forest, where she meets the sage and poet Valmiki, who gives her shelter. She tells him her story, from the beginning. In the seclusion of the forest, she bears twin sons who, when they are about fifteen years old, wander back to Ayodhya. There they enter the presence of the king, and Rama recognizes their likeness to him and the signs of their noble birth. Only then does he formally accept Sita back as his queen.

Well. I was taught that this was, indeed, a happy ending. Rama had put the welfare of his people, the need for an irreproachable monarch, above his own personal happiness and was rewarded by the reunion with his one great love and the blessings of the gods. In Laos I began to recognize the full reasons for the drastic change in emphasis that the more equitable and compassionate Laotians saw fit to put upon the teachings and the story of the *Ramayana.*

To them, Rama is far from a model of virtue, destined to be an incarnation of Vishnu, one of the basic triumvirate (with Siva and Brahma) of Hinduism. To them, not without justification, he is a preachy stick of a man, quite unfairly endowed with supernatural and godlike powers.

Ravana, on the other hand, appears to the Laotians to have shown commendable enterprise and ingenuity in capturing Sita. They feel that Sita is not altogether displeased at her predicament, and after all, doesn't Ravana treat her in a truly royal fashion? Could any woman ask for more admiration, cherishing, or lavishing of gifts and attention? And even though she is the helpless captive of the Demon King of Lanka, does he not behave in a most gentlemanly way toward her? He doesn't seduce her or rape her; he respects her wishes and would take her only if she were freely willing to accept his advances. And see how scrupulous he is about observing the military code with Hanuman—he could easily have had the monkey killed and avoided ruin. Besides all this, Ravana had acquired his princely position in a most worthy manner. He had so impressed the gods by his years of prayer, meditation, and asceticism that they had granted him magical powers and a kind of immortality: immunity from fatal attack by gods, devils, or the spirits of air, earth, or water; rashly, they had omitted mortal man from the list.

The Laotians do not actually change the outcome of the classic battle, although Rama's victory clearly seems to them unjust, supported as it was by the power of the gods and by the supernaturally invested strength of the monkeys. But they extend the story of the war as long as they can before they reluctantly, and with no sense of triumph, bring it to its traditional conclusion.

In the account of the reunion of Rama and Sita, however, they do make reckless changes to suit their sense of fair play. Shocked and disgusted by Rama's heartlessness in subjecting Sita to an ordeal by fire, they show Sita as equally repelled and outraged by his lack of trust in her innocence.

Sita had originally been a foundling. A king had come upon her as a tiny baby lying in a plowed field. Assuming that she had been entrusted to him by the deity and that her mother must be the goddess of the earth, he had named the baby Sita, meaning "furrow." He had taken great care of her and brought

TEXT CONTINUED ON PAGE 45

THE RAMAYANA IN PICTURES

Though born in India, the *Ramayana* belongs to what has been called the "collective dream" of all Southeast Asia. Not only does each of India's peoples possess its own version in its own language; so, too, do the predominantly Buddhist Burmese, Thais, Cambodians, and Laotians, as well as the Moslem Malays and Indonesians. The paintings on the following pages, here reproduced for the first time, are illustrations from a mid-nineteenth-century manuscript containing a version from the Punjab, in northern India: each of the paintings depicts an episode of Rama's long and complicated story.

On the facing page the central character is the female demon Shurpanaka. Having vainly courted Rama, exiled prince of Ayodhya, and then his brother Lakshmana, she has concluded that both love Sita, and in a jealous fury has tried to kill her; Lakshmana has cut off her nose and ears. Now, she seeks vengeance on all three, first by a frontal attack (top), and next by invoking the aid of her brother Khara (bottom). When these attempts fail, she persuades another brother, the demon king Ravana, to fly north from his capital in Lanka—presumably Ceylon—in pursuit of Sita (the scene at the top of page 44). Ravana carries off Sita and takes her back to Lanka as his prisoner. After a long search, Rama and Lakshmana find out where she is; their monkey allies then build a causeway to Ceylon (pages 42–43) and Rama, crossing it, storms Ravana's capital and defeats him. Returning to Ayodhya, Rama is at last enthroned as its rightful king (page 44, bottom).

While Lakshmana guards Sita, at right, Rama, the archer, repels an attack by demons seeking to avenge Shurpanaka, who is flying off at top left.

Shurpanaka (left center) asks her demon brother Khara, who is sitting cross-legged and with a donkey's head and horns, to help avenge her.

Rama's beloved Sita having been kidnapped and imprisoned in Ceylon, Rama's hordes of soldier-monkeys build a giant causeway from India to

Ceylon, across a rolling, demon-ridden sea. At left, Rama (dark) and his brother (light) hold a council of war, planning how they will attack Ravana.

Ten-headed Ravana travels from Ceylon in a flying chariot (twice shown), past a divine bird, Garuda (left), and many rishis, *beings who live in trees.*

Returning home after fourteen years of frenetic exile, Rama (center) is enthroned and crowned king of Ayodhya, to the cheers of his monkey allies.

TEXT CONTINUED FROM PAGE 40

her up with all the advantages of a princess, knowing that the agricultural prosperity of his kingdom depended on his cherishing the child.

In at least one version of the *Ramayana,* after Rama allowed Sita to return to her royal position, he still insisted (in spite of the incontrovertible evidence that the looks and bearing of his sons supplies) on summoning an enormous assembly before which Sita must publicly declare her innocence. Facing this new ordeal, the modest Sita invokes the Earth to attest to the truth of her statement by giving a sign to the gathered multitude. The Earth gave the ultimate in indignant motherly signs. She simply opened up and embraced her daughter with love, removing her forever from the power of unreasonable men. To the Laotians, at least, this seems the only proper ending, the only reasonable penalty for Rama for putting his Public Image before the word of his incomparably beautiful, loving, and irreproachable wife.

In other parts of Southeast Asia, and even in India, the ending of the story in Ayodhya takes on forms and colorations that happen to suit varying traits of character or concepts of morality. One similar account adds a postscript redeeming Rama, showing him heartbroken and tormented with longing for his lost Sita. Even the gods feel they must be merciful to a man in such remorse and distress of spirit. The form their mercy takes is a curious one—interpret it as cynically or as compassionately as your nature dictates. They send him Time, disguised as an ascetic who, in the Hindu code, has access to any household or personage, however grand. Time offers Rama two choices, with the stipulation that he *must* accept one of them: he can either stay on earth in unrelieved and isolated splendor as the revered, though companionless, monarch of his realm, or he can ascend to heaven to rule over the gods.

I suppose you would have to know at least a little about the quarrelsomeness, unpredictability, jealousy, capriciousness, unexpected kindness and co-operation, and equally sudden venomousness and cruelty the Hindu pantheon displays in its interminable and checkered activities and confrontations in order to grasp the enormity of this decision.

But we will never know what Rama's decision might have been, for it is at this precise moment that an irascible but extremely powerful sage arrives to see him. The caller threatens frightful curses—and traditionally, nothing is to be more dreaded than a Brahman's curses—if he is not given an audience *at once.* Lakshmana, who receives the sage, knows that to interrupt an interview with Time carries, without exception, the penalty of death. Still, to save Rama from the sage's curses, and possibly also from having to make his dire decision, he interrupts the conference with Time. He then walks peacefully to the riverside to wait for his own death. Much moved by this noble self-sacrifice, the gods shower him with garlands and lift him up into heaven to join their company.

Rama's death may seem more morally equivocal. He commits suicide. As one version describes it, "With great dignity and ceremony he walked into the river Sarayu, where Brahma's voice welcomed him from heaven and he entered into the 'glory of Vishnu,'" becoming Vishnu's seventh incarnation.

Considering the long, expansive, and complicated history of the actual epic, it isn't difficult to understand why the *Ramayana* is open to a number of diverse, often contradictory, interpretations. Scholars differ widely on sources, origins, and dates, but there are a few points on which they agree.

It seems likely, for instance, that the *Mahabharata* was, to some extent, based on actual occurrences during the first of the Aryan invasions of India from the north, and that it, as well as the *Ramayana,* chronicles (however imaginatively) the dynasties of that historical period. The traditional date for the great war that took place on the battlefield of Kurukshetra, described in the *Mahabharata,* is 3102 B.C. The sequence of kings and the relationships of principalities as they grew up seem, even in their legendary form, to follow a logical and unbroken pattern.

Unquestionably, the earliest recountings of these historical events were handed down in the spoken language, Sanskrit, by storytellers—a tradition of oral communication of history and literature that still continues in India. It is equally certain that incidents and characters, details of personality, points of view, and descriptions were modified, dramatized, or simply changed to suit the mood or feeling of the narrator or the temper and wishes of a particular audience.

For the *Ramayana* there is further and more recent evidence of the historical movements and wars on which it may have been based. The Aryans expanded into the peninsula of south India about 800 B.C., and some scholars maintain that the army of monkeys who helped Rama in his invasion of Ceylon were a symbolic depiction of south India's original Dravidian inhabitants—smaller in build than the Aryans, darker of skin and hair, agile, and with their own kingdoms. This would suggest that the earliest version of the *Ramayana* might have been composed fifty or a hundred years later.

What seems more likely is that the story, passed on for centuries by word of mouth, was eventually recorded by Valmiki, or a poet assuming that name, who permitted himself the license of involving himself in the action and of writing the extraordinary poem—24,000 *slokas,* or 48,000 sixteen-syllable lines, divided into seven books—as if he had personally been the recipient of the classic tale and was committing it to writing for all humanity.

He couldn't have known that while Sanskrit would become a dead language, the story would continue to spread and grow and would be translated into dozens of regional Indian languages—it is his version of the *Ramayana* with which most Indians are

45

familiar. Even as early as about A.D. 80 the fame of the *Ramayana* had spread to the West as well. Dion Chrysostom, the Greek scholar, wrote that "even among the Indians, they say, Homer's poetry is sung, having been translated by them into their own dialect and tongue." It is charitably assumed that he must have meant that epics similar to Homer's had a wide currency in India.

The *Ramayana* was to spread well beyond the boundaries of India. From about the sixth century A.D. on, Indian religion and culture expanded east and south, covering the islands (except for the Philippines) and the mainland of Asia until it reached the frontiers of influence of that other great Asian cultural giant, China, in Vietnam. All through Southeast Asia the *Ramayana* was to be learned, embellished on, enlarged, or abbreviated; it would find its way into songs and ballads and into dance dramas such as the Ram Lila or the great repertoire of the Kathakali of India; it would be adapted for Indonesian puppet plays and carved in exquisite bas-reliefs around the walls of Angkor Wat in Cambodia, in what Benjamin Rowland has described as "a continuous stone tapestry."

In Southeast Asia, even after successive waves of military, religious, and cultural invasions converted some of the peoples of Islam and others to Buddhism (the tiny island of Bali is now the only Hindu country outside India), the power of the old epics has proved invincible. Devoutly Moslem audiences in Java watch all-night shows of their fanciful leather puppets acting out, in silhouette on a white screen, their favorite portions of the story. Buddhist Cambodians, seeing the huge *Ramayana* cast of characters, all with typical Khmer faces, on their temples and monuments, still feel a prideful ownership of the epic. In Laos or Thailand, both Buddhist countries, children watching village performances by strolling companies enthusiastically join in the action of the great ten-day war, gamboling with the monkeys and using

Beside the Ganges, a professional storyteller, above, narrates parts of the Ramayana. Opposite, Balinese villagers, all men, sway and chant in the dance of the monkey warriors.

small sticks and stones to represent the forest trees and Himalayan boulders with which Hanuman's army built Rama's Bridge.

And wherever you travel in India, you are certain to find reminders of the *Ramayana*, as casual as a passing reprimand to a child ("Would Rama have disobeyed his father?") or as profound as the inspired dedication that went into the carving of the sculptures of the great Kailasa rock temple at Ellora.

Late one full-moon night last summer, I went with some friends to a tiny enclave of eleventh-century India oddly preserved at one edge of the huge, sprawling, modern city of Bombay. It used to be a fishing village called Banganga, and although the Big Town with its concrete office buildings and high-rise apartment houses has overtaken it, Banganga still retains its character. There is no road to Banganga. You can reach it only by walking along the rocky seashore of Bombay Island, or by a long flight of shallow steps leading down from the thickly built-up hill behind it. In Banganga there is a sacred tank, and at the far end of the tank, the temple of Walkeshwar, the Sand Lord.

By that hour the stalls of Banganga's miniature bazaar were closed, and some shrouded figures slept on the ground between them. The only light,

apart from the moon glittering and rippling on the water, came from the charcoal fire that glowed within the temple. And the only noise, above the pervasive whispering of the sea, was the chanting, punctuated by bells and cymbals and drums.

We sat down on the worn steps surrounding the tank to listen. On such nights, devotees gather at the temple to recite the *Ramayana*, all the way through, for the sake of one tiny episode embedded in the proliferous mythology that blossomed from the epic. On the long journey Rama and Lakshmana took through India in their search for Sita, the legend (in Bombay, at least) is that they stopped to rest on the beach at Banganga. There Rama, in his pious way, modeled from the wet sand a lingam, the phallic symbol that represents Siva. He worshiped before it, and his prayers were so fervent that Siva offered Rama a favor. The two brothers, tired and thirsty, and finding no fresh water on the island of Bombay, humbly asked for water.

Siva then told Rama to shoot an arrow into the air, and at the place where it returned to earth, a spring would gush out—but not an ordinary spring, for, miraculously, the water would come from the sacred river Ganges, a thousand miles away, and would always remain pure. This is how the temple tank, and that obscure little corner of Bombay got its name: *ban* (arrow), *Ganga* (the Indian name for the Ganges). And yet, it *is* unusual to find fresh water so close to the ocean. And yes, people do still drink from the tank with no apparent ill effects. I am sure there are perfectly adequate scientific explanations of this minor phenomenon, but as far as the local people are concerned, Banganga will remain Rama's reward from Siva for his piety, and his legacy to the present-day Indians who live there.

Thanks to her many books and articles on India, Santha Rama Rau may be our best-known interpreter of her homeland. She also teaches at Sarah Lawrence College.

JEAN RENOIR'S
LA GRANDE ILLUSION

World War I finished off the idea that dying for one's country was an aristocratic duty—and finished off the aristocrats who thought so. On this theme Renoir and a masterfully chosen cast made their classic film

Since 1938, when it was first shown in the United States, Jean Renoir's famous film has been mistitled. It is called *Grand Illusion*, but the French title is *La Grande Illusion*, and as every high-school student knows, this means *The Big Illusion*. The point is important, because the proper title avoids an opening note of half-romantic, lofty regret.

There is scarcely a list of great films, long or short, that does not include this one. I saw it when it was first shown here and have seen it many times since, and I can testify that it exemplifies an ancient truth: good art survives because as we change, it can change with us.

In the winter of 1936–1937, when *La Grande Illusion* was made, in the world of the Spanish Civil War, of Mussolini and Hitler gulping down the West, of Japan ravaging China, the film was a warning of the futility of war in the face of growing wars, an anatomy of the upheaval of 1914–1918 to show contemporaries how grim machineries had been set in motion. Today its pacifist intent, as such, seems somewhat less salient (though no less moving) because so many more human beings know how futile war is and know, too, that no film can abolish it.

Today the film seems a hard perception of inevitabilities, not glibly cynical but, in the largest classical sense, pessimistic: a film that no longer asks for action but that *accompanies* us, noting our best, prepared for our worst. Since

Erich von Stroheim was the German commander in La Grande Illusion, *filmed in 1937. Opposite, this 1967 photograph of Jean Renoir was taken by Henri Cartier-Bresson.*

this state of mind, this undepressed pessimism, is now widespread, this film continues to speak, out of the change it incorporates, to changing man.

Yet—in a wonderful and important way—*La Grande Illusion* is a period piece, and Renoir was the ideal maker for it. The history of film is full of remarkable confluences. D. W. Griffith came along just when the newborn me-

dium needed a genius to formulate its language. Eisenstein and Pudovkin came along in the Soviet Union just when the new society needed new artists to celebrate it in this new form. Six hundred years of Renaissance humanism, predictably ripening to decline, found a film elegist in a Frenchman born and nourished in its center, the son of a painter who had given *la belle époque* some of its humane and sensual loveliness.

Jean Renoir, son of Pierre Auguste, was born in 1894 in Paris. He has written a biography called *Renoir, My Father*, which inevitably contains a good deal about himself. In 1913 the young Renoir enlisted in the cavalry, and in 1915 he was wounded in the leg. (He still limps.) In 1916, after his recovery, he became a pilot in a reconnaissance squadron. (Maréchal, a leading character in *La Grande Illusion*, is a reconnaissance pilot who is wounded.) When the war ended, Renoir worked in ceramics for about five years, then in 1923 he began to write and direct films. By the mid-1930's he was one of the eminent directors of France, having made such highly regarded films as *Boudu Saved from Drowning, The Crime of Monsieur Lange*, and an adaptation of Gorki's *The Lower Depths*, and was well launched on a career that, whatever one's opinion of individual works, has as a whole had a huge influence on the later film world.

By STANLEY KAUFFMANN

1. 2. 3.

It would have been impossible for the man who made those early films to be unconcerned with what he saw happening in Europe and Asia and Africa in the mid-1930's. Renoir prepared to make *La Grande Illusion*, based on a story that he says "is absolutely true and was told to me by some of my comrades in the war." This combination—of authenticity and of response to a sense of historical twilight—roots the film firmly in its period, using the best of an age to bid that age farewell.

To collaborate on the script with him, Renoir engaged Charles Spaak, one of those important film figures of whom the public knows little, like Carl Mayer in the German 1920's and Cesare Zavattini in the Italian 1950's —the screenwriters who contributed greatly to celebrated eras. Spaak, the brother of Paul Henri Spaak, the former Belgian prime minister, wrote a

Omission as effect: Maréchal (Jean Gabin) scratches at the wall of his cell (1), distracts the guard's attention (2), and bolts out. The camera does not follow him but waits until the half-conscious prisoner is dragged back (4) and flung down (5).

number of memorable screenplays in a long career. By this time he had already written *La Kermesse Héroique (Carnival in Flanders)* for Jacques Feyder and the Gorki adaptation for Renoir.

This Spaak-Renoir screenplay tells the story of three French officers who are captured by the Germans and of one German officer who is their jailer. The drama is built in three sections. The first, after a brief prologue, takes place in an internment camp where the three Frenchmen try to tunnel to freedom but are transferred before the tunnel is ready. The second is in a fortress-prison, run by the German officer whom we met in the prologue, from which two of the Frenchmen escape with the help of the third. The last section is set in a German farmhouse where the two fugitives are sheltered for a time by a young widow who has a small daughter. And there is an epilogue, balancing the prologue, in which the two fugitives finally cross into Switzerland.

The movement of the film is thus toward freedom; but that freedom implies return to other "prisons," of

renewed military service or other straitenings of society. The officers' characters are unashamedly selected for contrast and symbolism—beginning with the fact that they are officers, not ordinary soldiers; but they are so well written, and played, that the effect is never of artifice, only of reality. Boeldieu is an aristocrat, a career officer; Maréchal is a mechanic, who might never have been an officer in an earlier, unmechanized war; Rosenthal is a Vienna-born Jew, whose parents emigrated to France, were naturalized, and prospered mightily (a distinct suggestion of the Rothschilds). The German is Rauffenstein, also an aristocrat, an aviator who shoots down the first two Frenchmen, entertains them to lunch before they go to prison camp, is himself subsequently shot down and maimed, and then reappears eighteen months later as the fortress commandant.

Maréchal and Rosenthal, both French, are parvenus of different sorts; Boeldieu and Rauffenstein, enemies, are both aristocrats and feel an affinity. War, says the film, is exclusively a matter of national loyalty only to nonprofessionals. To the international officer

1. 2. 3.

caste, national loyalty is a matter of honor, but, of course, loyalty is only one aspect of chivalry.

For the role of the French aristocrat, Renoir got Pierre Fresnay, formerly of the Comédie Française and a member of the Compagnie des Quinze under the famous Michel Saint-Denis. Maréchal was played by the rapidly rising Jean Gabin, who had already played for Renoir in *The Lower Depths* and was becoming a premier representative on the screen of the French working class. Marcel Dalio, an alumnus of the Paris Conservatory and of revues, already a film veteran, played Rosenthal. The German widow was played by the diminutive Dita Parlo, best known until then as the bride in *L'Atalante,* the only feature film made by the greatly gifted and prematurely deceased Jean Vigo. And in one of the masterstrokes of casting in film history, Rauffenstein was played by Erich von Stroheim.

This fascinating man came from cloudy beginnings. One biography says that he was born in Vienna in 1885, resigned a commission in the Austrian army in 1909 to emigrate to America, served a hitch in the U.S. cavalry, and

then held a wide variety of jobs. He broke into films under D. W. Griffith as a stunt man in *The Birth of a Nation.* He acted monocled German officers in Hollywood during the war and became publicized as "the man you love to hate." He went on to write and direct and play in such films as *Blind Husbands* and *Foolish Wives,* which, though they were rococo melodramas, were made with visual splendor and sardonic "Continental" realism. In 1924 he made *Greed,* from the Frank Norris novel *McTeague,* which is generally held to be one of the best films ever made in the United States but which helped to seal Stroheim's fate as a prodigal and "difficult" director.

After a rocky Hollywood career, he went to France as an actor, in 1936, to find himself the object of a cult. (Renoir himself has said that he saw *Foolish Wives* twelve times and that it opened his eyes about film-making.) To *La Grande Illusion* Stroheim brought the right physique and temperament and age and experience, but he also brought an immense and exactly apposite mystique. His presence in the picture is so forceful that when Richard Griffith re-

Prison life: Planning an amateur theatrical, the French POW's unpack a box of costumes (1) and a youth tries on a gown and wig (2, 3). The men laugh but each is moved by this hint of femininity (4). The camera pulls back as loneliness sweeps the room.

viewed it (*The Nation,* October 22, 1938), he didn't begin with Renoir; his opening line was: "It is unkind of Erich von Stroheim to debunk war's illusions in this graceless year."

The film immediately sets its tone with rhetorical devices that are used throughout: irony and ellipsis. Maréchal, in a French army officers' mess, has a date with a girl but is suddenly ordered to take Boeldieu on a reconnaissance flight; the date, instead of being postponed a few hours, is ironically postponed a few years, if not forever, because they are shot down. The sequence in the French officers' mess cuts immediately to the German officers' mess. Ellipsis: we don't see the air fight. (We never see any battle in this war film.) Irony: the German officers' mess, save for a few details, is just like the French one.

In the first camp—let us call it Act

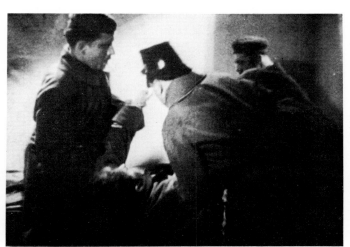

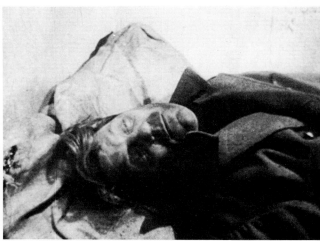

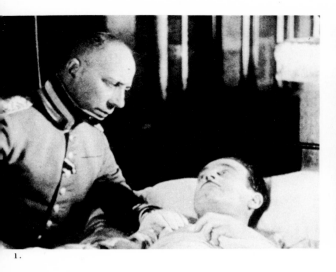

1.

2.

3.

One—we live with Boeldieu, the gentleman officer who keeps his white gloves fresh in prison, who says he has always called his wife and mother *vous*, yet who insists on doing his part in the dirty tunnel-digging. Maréchal is the *homme moyen*, but his self-knowledge of this—without self-dramatization—keeps the character from being stock. Among the other officers in the barracks are a teacher and an actor, but the most interesting is Rosenthal, the wealthy Jew.

Consider that this role was written in 1936, when the Nazis were already tormenting Jews in Germany and when anti-Semitic feeling was simmering in France and even in Britain; consider, too, that Renoir is unquestionably among the most humane of men, and your admiration grows for his insistence on drawing Rosenthal with hon-

Common man's survival: Maréchal and Rosenthal bid good night to Elsa (1), who has sheltered them, and retire (2). Maréchal pauses (3), sees Elsa through a doorway (4), and goes to embrace her (5). Maréchal and the camera have moved in a circle, underscoring the scene's emotional content.

esty, instead of making him a saintly martyr as counterpropaganda against the times. Rosenthal is a decent enough fellow who wants to "belong" and who knows he doesn't "belong" completely, who is rich and will not hide it, in fact who boasts as proof of his "Frenchness" that his family owns a nice chunk of France. His family sends him big parcels of good food, which the Germans pass because they then have to give less food to that barracks. And Rosenthal uses these parcels as a means to be accepted.

In short, Rosenthal is a good image of the risen bourgeois European Jew, rather proud of all these facts, yet seeking to blend into a national landscape, morally no better or worse than most others, aware that he is tolerated, anxious to *be* tolerated, and willing to pay for it, on the implied ground that it is better to have purchased acceptance than to have none at all.

Thus we have in this barracks a model of European society, with all major strands represented except the peasant/worker—who was excluded arbitrarily because this is an officers' camp. We know, as we watch, that we

are being shown a model, but it is made with such fine observation and dexterity—and, to repeat, is so well performed—that it rings with truth.

Two scenes, particularly, from Act One are notable. Rosenthal gets a basket of costumes from home for a camp show. A boyish officer goes inside to try on a dress and female wig. When he comes out—uneffeminately—silence gradually spreads around the big, crowded room. Memory and loneliness float over the men's heads, and make them still.

After the camp show, Maréchal is put in solitary for insulting the German command. He sits torpidly in his cell, picking idly at the stone wall with a spoon. When his guard comes in to talk with him, he goes berserk and rushes out through the open door. The camera does *not* go with him; it waits patiently with the guard until, very shortly, the subdued Maréchal is carried back into the cell by other German soldiers. (Another ellipsis.)

A second German guard exemplifies another system of Renoir's—the crystallized vignette. This guard is a middle-aged, round-shouldered man.

1.

2.

3.

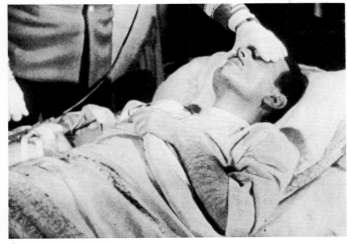

His very appearance tells us of the man-power drain in Germany, his manner tells us that he, too, is imprisoned. Whenever I see *La Grande Illusion,* I wait for this man's brief appearance, as I wait for the haughty English officer who grinds his watch under his boot to keep the Germans from getting it, and the owl-eyed, frightened orderly who attends Rauffenstein in his castle.

When we get to the castle—Act Two —more elements are joined. The reappearance of Rauffenstein, now in a neck brace and invalided out of action, is a trenchant signal of the passage of time: it not only indicates how the war is wearing on and on, it seems to give the film itself a lengthening perspective, a sense of experience and journey. The quick affinity between the German and Boeldieu broadens the social fabric by internationalizing the officer set; and dramaturgically, it gives each of them someone to whom he can talk easily. It allows them to comment on the passing of the class paradigms, centuries old, that made their very existence. However, as a gentleman, Boeldieu never derogates his fellow officers to Rauffenstein. Clearly it is Rauffen-

stein, the jailer, who needs these conversations more than Boeldieu, the prisoner. (Another irony.)

The culminating irony of Act Two is the escape of Maréchal and Rosenthal, made possible by the decoy act of Boeldieu—the past recognizes that its last function is to make the future possible. Boeldieu climbs a parapet and plays a tune on a flute to distract the guards, and the irony is heightened when it is Rauffenstein himself, the other aristocrat, who shoots him when he refuses to come down.

The act ends with Boeldieu's death, surely one of the most masterly scenes ever filmed. He lies in Rauffenstein's room in great pain; the maimed German, the man who shot him, sits beside him, apologizing for his poor aim yet envying the other aristocrat his death in war. The nurse ends the conversation. Rauffenstein goes to a cabinet and pours a drink. The nurse calls him softly. He knows what has happened. Without turning, he takes the drink. Then, after closing Boeldieu's eyes, he cuts a geranium from a flower pot, which we know is the only flower in the fortress.

Aristocrat's death: Rauffenstein (1) sits beside Boeldieu, whom he has been forced to shoot; he turns briefly away to pour a drink (2) but is summoned by the nurse (3) and closes the dead man's eyes (4). Numbly he cuts the blossom from his geranium (5), the only flower growing in the prison fortress.

If the film ended here, with Boeldieu dead and Rauffenstein envious of him, with Maréchal and Rosenthal making their way through the snowy countryside to the border, it would in fact be a complete work, but of smaller dimension than it finally attains. Renoir is dealing not only with the past but with the future, not only with symbols of war but with war itself as a symbol of the world in which war happens.

The two fugitives trudge through the snow in mufti, which was part of their escape equipment. Rosenthal limps. He has sprained his ankle, and it keeps getting worse. His condition irritates Maréchal, and in a few days they quarrel. He says he never liked Jews anyway, and Rosenthal says he ought to have thought of that earlier. Maréchal stomps off alone, and Rosenthal sits on a rock, singing defiantly. His song

1.   2.

breaks off as (an ellipsis again) Maréchal suddenly reappears quietly. We
have not seen him change his mind, we
do not hear him apologize. We know
he really does have anti-Semitism in
him and that Rosenthal knows it and is
prepared to live with it because he
knows that Maréchal regrets having it
—all this in Maréchal's silent reappearance at the edge of the frame.

The two men take refuge in a barn,
where they are discovered by the
owner, Elsa, a young widow. Her
losses in the war—her husband and her
brothers—have purged her of fear,
even of hate. They stay with her until
Rosenthal recovers, and they make a
pet of Elsa's small daughter. Maréchal
helps around the farm, and this leads
to the film's one really bad scene. As he
feeds the cow one day, he says to it:
"You don't mind being fed by a French-

*Crossing the border: The fugitives have
reached the Swiss frontier (1); they say their
farewell (2) lest they be killed in flight. The
camera pans to border patrolmen (3), who
take aim (4) but too late. The Frenchmen have
fled—from prison, Germany, and (for the
moment) war. The camera watches them go.*

man. . . . You're just a poor cow, and
I'm just a poor soldier." How I wish
that this heavily explicit scene had
been omitted.

Maréchal and Elsa become lovers,
but when Rosenthal's ankle is better,
the two men must leave for the border.
Maréchal tells Elsa that after the war,
if he is not killed, he will come back for
her and the child and take them to
France. Both he and Elsa believe it
equally: that is, they both know he
really means it—at the moment. This
is one more belief that (we feel) will be
turned into illusion by the passage of
time, like the larger beliefs of class and
of war-with-a-purpose.

In the last scene, the epilogue, the
two Frenchmen are standing in the
snow, bidding farewell to one another
before they try to cross a long valley to
the border. Embracing, they call each
other affectionately by the names that
they have used angrily before. Then
they start. A German border patrol
spots them and fires a few times, but
they have made it into Switzerland. In
the last long shot we see two small figures struggling through the snow toward a village. Toward repatriation.

Toward return to the war. Toward
some sort of life and some sort of death.

Enriching, supporting, fulfilling all
the above, is, fundamentally, Renoir's
direction, his sheerly cinematic abilities. His skill with actors shines from
every scene (he has been an actor himself), but two qualities of his filmic
style are especially important: his use
of a moving camera and his deep-focus
composition.

An example of the way he moves his
camera. When Maréchal arrives in his
first prison barracks, we see him in a
close two-shot with a fellow prisoner, a
former actor, talking about the theatre.
As they continue to converse, the camera gently pulls back, disclosing Boeldieu and others also conversing in the
large room, and *the camera itself* tells
us that Maréchal is being integrated
into a new community.

Deep-focus is somewhat more complex. Put much too simply, one can say
there are two general approaches to
film-making. First, the montage approach, developed by Eisenstein and
Pudovkin and others, out of Griffith,
which relies on joining bits of film together in rhythmic and pictorial rela-

The woods a[...] and in the
valley we'll g[...] all fours.

1.   2.   3.

4.

tionships so that an effect is created out of the very way the pieces are joined, an effect additional to the effects of the separate bits, just as an arpeggio is an entity in itself made up of separate musical entities.

In the deep-focus approach the reliance is on the content of any one shot, rather than on a succession of shots. (The shot may be one in which the camera moves; it is the absence of cutting that makes the real difference.) The French film critic André Bazin praised Renoir because he "uncovered the secret of a film form that would permit everything to be said without chopping the world up into little fragments, that would reveal the hidden meaning in people and things without disturbing the unity natural to them."

One point that Bazin and other deep-focus theorists have generally disregarded is that this deep-focus principle is about twenty-five hundred years old and is usually called "the theatre." Renoir, who has written and directed plays, simply combined the flow of cinema with the relationships within a frame that are standard practice in the theatre.

One example. Maréchal and Rosenthal are in the farmyard, and the former says he hasn't the courage to tell Elsa that they must leave. Rosenthal agrees to do it, goes into the house, and delivers the message. Elsa nods and disappears. Then Rosenthal opens the curtained window and we see Maréchal, still where he was, out there in the yard leaning on a fence. The opening of that window, suddenly deepening the screen, the addition of that plane to the composition, creates a tension between Maréchal outside and what has just happened in the room—a device often used in the theatre by lifting a drop or lighting up a dark area.

Today the Big Illusion of the title includes at least three aspects: the illusion that war accomplishes anything; the illusion that, even without war, men will be brothers; and the illusion that truth can ever be anything more than a necessary illusion. Yet the presentation of all these illusions is here in the hands of a man committed to love.

In his book about his father Renoir says that when he and his brother were children, his parents often went to the theatre, leaving them in the care of a

The leave-taking: The escaped prisoners must make their break for France. Maréchal (1) sends Rosenthal to tell Elsa good-bye (2). Embarrassed, he opens the window (3), revealing Maréchal outside (4). This is an example of Renoir's deep-focus technique —the addition of a new plane to the screen.

neighbor. Nevertheless, his parents would jump in a cab at intermission and rush home for a few minutes to make sure the children were all right. A child who has known a home like that must grow up to inevitable disappointments, but is secure against them. For the characters in *La Grande Illusion,* their figurative parents—the traditions and ideals of the past—will not be back at intermission; they will never be back. The film is a farewell to their memory and an acceptance of a world without them.

La Grande Illusion can be rented, in 16 mm. form, from Janus Films, 745 Fifth Avenue, New York, New York 10022. French dialogue, English subtitles. A paperbound edition of the screenplay, in very British English, is available from Simon and Schuster.

The Shooting of Captain Speke

The two most famous explorers of their day were to engage that afternoon in fierce debate. Where was the source of the Nile? Each man thought he knew. But as Sir Richard Burton waited for his rival to appear, the terrible news was announced

On September 16,1864, the English spa of Bath, in Somerset, awoke in a state of pleasurable, if slightly shamefaced, anticipation. Long past its prime as a fashionable resort, its prevailing tone was set now by retired military men and colonial administrators, and the walls of its ancient abbey were crowded with memorials to the genteel departed. As a wit wrote of them,

These walls, so full of monument and bust,
Show how Bath's waters serve to lay the dust.

Bath's glorious Georgian squares and crescents, which made it one of the handsomest cities in Europe, were mostly peeled and shabby, and petered away into the countryside in half-completed speculations, abandoned since the end of the spa's eighteenth-century boom. The old place had subsided into provincial respectability and had acquired a name for seedy dullness that was to persist for another century.

September of 1864, nevertheless, was a gala month for Bath. The British Association for the Advancement of Science, founded thirty years earlier to foster public interest in the sciences, was holding its annual conference there. Savants and enthusiasts had ar-

John Hanning Speke, sportsman and explorer, is portrayed with sextant and shotgun by the cataract of Lake Victoria, ultimate source of the Nile, which he discovered in 1862.

Sir Richard Burton

rived from all over the kingdom, and at a moment when applied science had reached the apogee of esteem, all educated eyes were turned to the proceedings at Somerset. The London newspapers carried long daily accounts, and the Bath *Chronicle* had imported forty typesetters from London to produce a daily newspaper that reported nothing else.

All the hotels and lodging houses were full. The more celebrated squares, parades, and terraces were alive with the comings and goings of the great, and the *Chronicle*'s social reporters (who continued until 1939 to record the arrival of hotel guests) could scarcely keep up with the soirées, concerts, balls and private dinner parties—over whose tables, between whose quadrilles, eminent men of science argued

the possibilities of a fifth dimension or discussed the anthropologic characteristics of the Lapps.

For the general public the greatest scientific excitement of the day was exploration. The urge to open up the world was inextricably linked with the emotions of Empire, just beginning to be a popular enthusiasm, and anything to do with foreign discovery aroused an avid interest. The Royal Geographical Society, a powerful force in the land, held its own annual conference as Section E (Geography and Ethnology) of the British Association, and down at Bath the real lions of the month were the celebrities returned from, or at least concerned with, exotic parts.

Henry Bates, the Amazon naturalist, was there, and Bishop Colenso, as famous for his knowledge of Zulu life as for his theological heresies, and J. M. Stuart, the first man to cross Australia from south to north, who was visibly and satisfyingly shattered by his terrible journey two years before. Dr. Livingstone was staying in appropriate splendor at No. 13, The Circus, one of the finest houses in Bath, attended wherever he went by adulatory crowds: and present, too, though less easily recognized, were influential figures on the fringe of the exploratory saga, like Sir Roderick Murchison, President of the R.G.S., or Sir William Armstrong of Newcastle, whose patented rifle kept

Speke, the passionate and expert hunter, fells an African buffalo.

the world, in a manner of speaking, safe for British adventure.

Bath that September, in fact, was like an analogue of the imperial momentum itself—the zest, the hero worship, the covert rivalries, the fascination of distant places and sensational goings-on, even the sanctimony: for as Dr. Livingstone told the mayor's banquet at the Guildhall, British discoveries were never selfishly hoarded but were "communicated to the world, and being known to the whole world were prevented from being lost."

But the sixteenth was an extra-special day. Among the celebrities in the city were the two most controversial figures of African exploration, Richard Burton and John Hanning Speke. They were enemies. Together they had gone to Africa to search for the source of the Nile River, the supreme prize of exploration. Speke claimed to have found the source during a solitary sortie, Burton doubted it, and the resulting quarrel had become public property.

They were theatrically contrasted antagonists. Speke, the scion of a well-known Somerset family, was an upstanding young Victorian gentleman of the middle rank, a sportsman to his finger tips, boyish and well spoken, his eyes frank, his ears slightly cauliflowered. Unmarried at thirty-seven, he was a local hero: his family home, Jordans, was only forty miles away, and he had relatives all over the county, including some on the outskirts of Bath.

Burton, on the other hand, could hardly have been more alien to the spa. He was the very antithesis of Victorian decorum. His eyes flamed, his black

mustaches drooped, he had a profound knowledge of Oriental pornography and was reputed to have done dreadful things in many remote corners of the world. He had made a famous journey in disguise to the forbidden places of Mecca and had also been the first European to penetrate the scarcely less alarming city of Harar in Ethiopia. A true scholar and a marvelous linguist —he had translated the Portuguese poet Camoëns—Burton had recently married a harebrained, fanatic but doting Catholic, Isabel Arundell, and he lived in a more or less constant condition of fury.

These two men had not met since their return from Africa in 1859, but the newspapers and learned journals reverberated with their differences. The insults and innuendoes had grown more vicious each year, and as a climax to it all the R.G.S. had arranged a formal confrontation between them, to take place at 3 P.M. on the sixteenth as part of Section E's proceedings. It was the prospect of this meeting that gave Bath its half-illicit thrill that morning. Anything, it was thought, might happen.

The improbable setting for the clash between the heroes was the Mineral Water Hospital. This was almost as forbidding as it sounds. The principal hospital of the spa, using (as the Romans did) the local hot springs for the treatment of rheumatic complaints, it had been built more than a century before and was squeezed with gloomy classicism into the city's narrow medieval center. Long ahead of time that afternoon its hall was packed, but as three

o'clock approached the eager audience began to sense that something was wrong. Only two people were on the platform—Burton himself, looking terrifyingly severe, and his plump, determined Isabel. None of the other dignitaries and celebrities were to be seen: Murchison, Livingstone, the members of the council, or Speke.

The minutes passed. The Burtons sat there awkwardly. The dour building brooded. The audience grew restive, giving vent to its impatience, the *Chronicle* reported, "by sounds more often heard from the audience of a theatre than of a scientific meeting." At last, twenty-five minutes late, Murchison walked slowly onto the platform, followed by his council and their distinguished guests. He was holding a note, and when the audience fell silent, he read it aloud. Captain Speke, he announced, was dead. He had been "missed in the field" while out shooting the day before and had been found "shot through the body close to the heart. He lived only a few minutes."

"By God," Burton is supposed to have exclaimed, collapsing into his chair, "he's killed himself."

For the origins of this tragedy we must go back to the moment, six years before, when Burton and Speke stood at the brink of that supreme geographic revelation, the discovery of where the Nile began.

The compelling fascination of the Nile had exerted itself upon empires in existence long before the British. Through the centuries historians, geographers, and romantics had propounded theories about its source, which had acquired in turn a fabulous, an intellectual, and a strategic meaning. The river was said to spring from "fountains" deep in the African interior, from a range of snow-capped peaks, from a system of great lakes, or from Ptolemy's Mountains of the Moon in Ethiopia. The source of the Blue Nile had been identified by the Scottish explorer James Bruce in 1770, but the greater stream, the White Nile, remained even in those days of Victorian enlightenment a total mystery.

Nobody knew where it came from. It was a superb enigma, and as the British responded to their imperial destiny, as the public began to acquire its proprietary interest in the other side of the horizon, as the London strategists evolved the theory that control of Egypt was essential to the security of British India, so the problem of the Nile became almost a national obsession. Like the ascent of Everest a century later, the British regarded it as a challenge specific to themselves, and its solution as the greatest prize awaiting any British adventurer of the time.

Burton and Speke were the first to make the attempt. By 1858 most of Africa was imperfectly understood. Kilimanjaro and Kenya had been seen. Much of the Niger had been navigated. The Kalahari had been penetrated. The mythical Timbuktu had been reached at last, and had proved a dreary fraud. The time was right, the pundits of the R.G.S. had thought, for a determined effort to reach the fountains of the Nile: so they commissioned Burton and Speke, both officers of the Indian army, to make the attempt from the east coast—the most direct route, it was assumed, and one whose lower course had been well established by generations of Arab slavers bringing their captives to Zanzibar for shipment. The two soldiers had already been in Africa together, on a disastrous expedition to Somaliland. Burton, at thirty-seven, was famous for his journey to Mecca: Speke, thirty-one, was unknown but ambitious.

One would have thought them incompatible from the start. Speke seems always to have been secretly, often resentfully, in awe of Burton. Most people were. Not only could his manner be scathing and his temper terrible, but his arrogance was based on such genuine accomplishments that it could not be shrugged off. He loved to argue, to disconcert, to outrage society and cock snooks at the Establishment. A rootless Anglo-Irishman, largely self-educated—Oxford got rid of him as soon as it could—he was hampered by no class conventions and reveled in the fabled exploits of his past, such as his alleged affair with a nun in Goa, or his well-known investigation of the homosexual brothels of Karachi. In Africa Burton despised the blacks, whom it was fashionable to befriend, and openly cultivated the wicked but urbane Arab slave traders.

All this left Speke dazzled, slightly shocked, and doubtless envious. He resented Burton's command, and probably felt inadequate in the presence of Burton's flamboyant and sardonic authority. Speke was, in externals at least, the quintessential English gentleman, whose family came to England with the Conquest and had been providing quintessential English gentlefolk ever since. He had proved his courage in the Sikh wars of the 1840's, and was a good shot, an able geologist, and a knowledgeable botanist—as one acquaintance described him, "a right good, jolly, resolute fellow."

Most people liked him on sight. They thought him modest and straightforward. Only those who knew him better realized that, by a paradox not uncommon in men of his kind, he was blessed with a powerful inner mysticism, like a divining rod of the mind, which urged him to instinctive actions and conclusions and fired him with an irrational zeal.

Relations between the two men had not been good since the Somali expedition, which Speke believed to have been mismanaged by Burton, and during the long journey through the African bush they got steadily worse. Burton had always felt the attraction of Speke, but there was no pretending they had much in common. Burton was bored with blood sports, Speke adored them. Burton was a profoundly intellectual man, Speke a gentlemanly philistine. Burton picked up languages like stones from the ground, Speke was no linguist. Speke believed with Livingstone that one of the purposes of exploration was the extension of the Christian ethos; Burton, himself a half-convinced Moslem, was almost alone among the public figures of the time in believing that Islam could do better.

In February, 1858, they became the first Europeans to set eyes on Lake Tanganyika, which Burton thought might be the Nile's source: but it seemed to lie too low, and had no apparent outlet. Exhausted and sick—Speke was almost blind with trachoma, Burton half-paralyzed by malaria—they returned to recuperate at the slave-trading settlement of Kazeh, now called Tabora, which stood at a crossroads of the slave routes. There the acquaintance was further strained, Burton delighting in the company of the unprincipled Arab grandees of the place, Speke, one feels, severely disapproving of them and suspecting them of vices worse than slaving. So Burton was only too pleased when Speke, his eyesight recovered, proposed to make a solitary sortie to the north, leaving Burton to work up his notes and get his strength back. They had heard of another, larger body of water, Ukerewe, or the Northern Lake, three weeks' journey away. Might this not be the source of the Nile? Early in July, Speke set off on muleback with twenty porters and thirty armed guards, determined to find out.

So the controversy began. Twenty-five days later, on August 3, 1858, Speke became the first European to reach what is now Lake Victoria Nyanza. It is easy to imagine why the experience had for him an apocalyptic quality. Set among rolling, scrubby downland interspersed with forests of dark green, speckled with little islands haunted by ibis in the daytime and fireflies by night, splashed with gay tropic colors of mango, orchid, and wavering bird, and rippled always by a warm African breeze, the lake remains even now a marvelous surprise. Two hundred and fifty miles long (almost as large as Scotland), it is really an inland sea, and in that country seems spectacularly out of place, like an error of creation, or at least an afterthought.

Speke has lately become a favorite victim for Freudian amateurs, and certainly his reactions to this grand vision invite analysis. First he shot a passing bird—as if (suggests his latest biographer, Alexander Maitland) "the brooding spirit with whom Speke held intensely private communion demanded a sacrifice of blood in return for its favours." Then he gave names to his discoveries: the hillock he stood upon he called Somerset, for his home county, the creek at his feet he called Jordans, after the paternal home, the lake he called Victoria Nyanza for the queen—herself, we are authoritatively told, a dream synonym for his own mother. He then went on to reach a dramatic, intuitive conclusion. He flatly decided, without further evidence, that this was the source of the Nile. He explored no more. He spent only three days on the lake. He spoke no local language. He saw no river outlet. Yet he *knew* that this was the beginning of the White Nile, and being now short of supplies, he hurried excitedly back to Kazeh to tell Burton.

His reception was caustic. "It was," Burton recorded dryly, "an inspiration perhaps.... The fortunate discoverer's conviction was strong; his reasons were weak." A local worthy had told Speke that Lake Victoria probably extended to the end of the world. "Strongly impressed by this statistical information," Burton commented in his best schoolmaster style, "my companion therefore planned the northern limit about 4°–5° degrees north lat." It was not that Burton dismissed Victoria as the main source of the Nile. It was Speke's irrational certainty that infuriated him, coupled no doubt with a nagging feeling that he had missed his own chance of glory by staying behind.

Like husband and wife at the end of a long day, they found they could not mention the subject without bickering, and so they returned laboriously and unhappily to the coast, sick, exhausted, and tired of each other. They had been in each other's company for nearly three years, and knew each other's every fault. When they got to Aden, it was agreed that Speke should go on to England at once and that Burton should follow a little later, when he had regained his strength. According to Burton, the parting was self-consciously cordial. "I shall hurry up, Jack," Burton said, "as soon as I can," and Speke is said to have replied: "Goodbye old fellow; you may be quite sure I shall not go up to the Royal Geographical Society until you come to the fore and we appear together. Make your mind quite easy about that."

But when Burton reached London, several weeks later, Speke's "discovery of the Nile's source" was already one of the excitements of the town. Speke had reported to the R.G.S. the very first day after his arrival. He had addressed a meeting of its members and had already been commissioned to take his own expedition back to Africa and confirm his conclusions. Burton arrived home almost disregarded in the aftermath of this triumph—"a mere skeleton," his wife recorded, "with brown-yellow skin hanging in bags, his eyes protruding, and his lips drawn away from his teeth." He must have been worth seeing, but nobody took much notice of him; the ground, he said, was "cut from under my feet." Speke was the man of the hour.

The squabble festered and brought out the worst in both of them. Burton retreated into bitter and often ill-judged sarcasm; Speke displayed an altogether unexpected streak of vindictive conceit. For the rest of their lives the two men never spoke to one another again, but their quarrel dragged on, attracting partisans on either side.

Now Speke, as it happened, was right. Against all the odds of probability, his emotional conviction on the shore of the Northern Lake was geographically correct. Two years later he was back in Africa with a very different companion, James Augustus Grant of the Indian army, who worshiped Speke with a spaniel-like devotion and would never dream of contradicting him. Once again, by design, accident, or instinct, Speke was alone when he reached Jinja, on the northern shore of Lake Victoria, and saw at last, on July 21, 1862, the Nile falling over its rim in cataract and rainbow. This time he had no qualms when he returned to camp and a waiting Grant. "Inform Sir Roderick Murchison that all is well," he cabled home as soon as he could, "and that the Nile is settled." Then he set off down the course of the river to Egypt, home, and glory.

So, in the end, it was to prove. Subsequent explorers were to demonstrate that the White Nile ran out of Lake Victoria into Lake Albert and was supplemented by water from various tributaries before it joined the Blue Nile at Khartoum and proceeded through Egypt to the Mediterranean. But to Speke's dismay, it was still *not* settled in 1863. Once again there was an intuitive element to his conviction. He had certainly proved that the Nile issued from Victoria, but in following it to Egypt he had taken one big short cut and had never circumnavigated the lake itself. It was perfectly possible that an even greater or higher source lay elsewhere. Speke and Grant returned to London to find that, though Queen and public received them as heroes, among the specialists there was doubt.

Theoretical geographers distrusted Speke's dogmatic assurance—brasher now, and tinged with a kind of tropical frenzy. Even the R.G.S., Speke's own sponsor, had new reservations. The young charmer of 1858 had soured with age. The meaner side of his character showed more often, and his narrowness of education, his country-squire philosophies, did not much endear him to the bookish world of science. He was a poor speaker, and he had developed an unhappy knack of antagonizing people. But he still had many supporters, just as Burton had a host of enemies, for the rift between the two had taken on new dimensions.

Each man represented a contemporary attitude toward Africa as a whole. Burton's approach was essentially scholarly: he was interested in Africa for its own sake, frequently contemptuous, often appalled, but neither censorious nor anxious to improve it. Speke's approach was more constructive. He believed it the Christian West's duty to reform the continent by trade and devout example, propagated by government-supported missionaries in the barbaric kingdoms of the interior.

Their antipathy was now irreconcilable, with that special bitterness that is tainted with lost intimacy. When, in the summer of 1864, the R.G.S. invited them both to debate the issue at Bath, a common acquaintance told Burton what Speke's reaction had been. If Burton appeared at Bath, Speke was reported to have said, "I will kick him." "Well," Burton replied, "that settles it. By God, he shall kick me!"

Burton and his wife characteristically put up at a hotel near the railway station, well off the fashionable round, but Speke, no less typically, stayed with his uncle, John Fuller, at his agreeable country house, Neston Park, which still stands hospitable and unaltered just over the Wiltshire border about ten miles from Bath. There can be little doubt as to which of the rivals felt the more assured. Burton was at the peak of his powers, wittier, more sardonic, and cleverer than ever. Speke, by contrast, was not only nervous but perhaps regretful: he had carried the enmity too far, and thus he placed himself at a moral as well as an intellectual disadvantage. Besides, in straight debate he would be horribly outclassed; incoherent before the friendliest of audiences, he was slightly deaf, had poor eyes, and was in a depressed condition, anyway.

They saw one another for the first time since 1859 at a preliminary meeting of Section E at the hospital on the day before the debate. It was a moment charged with unexpected pathos, if we are to believe Isabel Burton's account. The two men did not speak, but their eyes met. "I shall never forget his face," wrote Isabel of Speke. "It was full of sorrow, and yearning, and perplexity. Then he seemed turned to stone." After a while, she reported, he began to fidget, and exclaiming half aloud, "Oh, I cannot stand this any longer," got up from his seat. "Shall you want your chair again, sir?" said a man standing behind. "May I have it? Shall you come back?" "I hope not," Speke said, and left the hall.

So, at least, Mrs. Burton described it. Certainly Speke left, and following the habit of a lifetime, drove out to Neston, up the steep Box Hill, past Brunel's famous railway tunnel, to let off steam with an afternoon's shooting. By two thirty, we are told, he and his cousin, George Fuller, with the gamekeeper Daniel Davis, were out in the fields looking for partridges.

Neston stands on an outcrop of the Cotswolds to the north, and the field where Speke died is a bleak place, stony, bare, and gray, where the autumn light is often moist and misty and the air is dank. Low, unmortared walls cross it, and on a hazy September afternoon the group of cottages that stand beyond look chilly and uninviting. It seems a very long way from the urbanities of Bath, but it was native ground for Speke. Not only was that field his uncle's property, but in a house just across the Bath road lived his elder brother, William, heir to Jordans. Speke had, in fact, hurried from Section E straight home to his roots: away from the word-splitting and the hypothetical, back to the rough, where a chap was not stifled by theories or twisted by recriminations but could breathe freely among his own kind, in good country air, with a gun under his arm.

According to George Fuller's later account, the three men were well apart as they crossed the field. Fuller was about sixty yards from Speke, and Davis was about two hundred yards from Fuller, marking birds. At about four o'clock a shot sounded. Speke was at that moment crossing a dry-stone wall two or three feet high, and others looked round to see him falling off it. They ran to the spot and found him bleeding severely from the chest. He was conscious and asked them not to move him: but by the time Fuller had got hold of a doctor and returned to the scene, Speke had died where he had fallen, watched by the helpless keeper.

The news did not reach Burton that night. Speke's body was taken to his brother's house, and an inquest was convened for the following day, the day of the great debate. When, next morning, the news was announced to Section E, even Burton was stunned for a moment. Unable, he said, to speak himself, he asked Murchison to read a statement on his behalf, expressing his "sincere admiration of Speke's character and enterprise," despite their differences of opinion.

Within a few moments, though, he had recovered sufficiently to read a paper he happened to have with him about the present state of Dahomey, in West Africa, with particular reference to the habit of human sacrifice. Isabel says that he spoke haltingly, and with a voice that trembled, but if we are to believe the Bath *Chronicle*, at least he stuck it out gamely.

"Captain Speke came to a bad end," Burton wrote to a friend five days later, "but no one knows anything about it." In Somerset, nevertheless, he was given the farewell appropriate to a hero and a favorite son. Mr. Hall of Bath was commissioned to take a death mask, and the corpse was buried in the family vault at Dowlish Wake near Ilminster, some forty miles from the spa. Muffled bells tolled all day in Ilminster and Taunton, the county seat; and Murchison, Livingstone, and Grant all went to the funeral—Grant, indeed, descending momentarily into the vault with the coffin, carrying a wreath of laurel leaves and white everlasting flowers and sobbing sobs "audible all over the sacred building." Speke's father was granted the right to augment the family arms with the "supporters following: that is to say, on the dexter side a Crocodile, and on the sinister side a Hippopotamus."

But how he really died remains obscure to this day. "The charitable say he shot himself," Burton wrote, "the uncharitable say that I shot him." Murder by Burton is certainly a tempting hypothesis. Burton was widely rumored to have murdered an Arab during his journey to Mecca, a legend he happily propagated by silence, and there is an undeniably persuasive *frisson* to the vision of the great pornographer, cloaked and satanic, skulking in the lee of the death wall that September afternoon. But he was not really the murdering kind. He loved to shock, not to kill. He was a generous man at heart, and moreover, he retained to the end a genuine if wry affection for Speke.

When he and his wife returned to their hotel that evening, so Isabel tells us, he wept bitterly, crying over and over again "Jack! Jack!" But Burton did not immediately moderate his attacks on Speke, and the argument he had intended to present at Bath he published in a nasty little book, *The Nile Basin,* which his best friends thought in bad taste. Yet in a later work, *Zanzibar,* he published a poem, ostensibly by Isabel, more probably by himself, that summed up his relationship with Speke in a tone of sentimental and even sensual regret:

Yet were we comrades for years and years,
    And endured in its troth our companionship
Through a life of chances, of hopes, and fears;
    Nor a word of harshness e'er passed the lip,
Nor a thought unkind dwelt in either heart,
    Till we chanced—by what chance did it hap?
    —to part.

It was Speke, not Burton, who was the man of violence. He it was who, confronted by emotional crises, relieved the strain by going out and killing something, and there were many besides Burton to assume, in September, 1864, that what he chose to kill that particular day was himself. The evidence at the inquest was, as might be expected, conciliatory—suicide was a great disgrace to a Victorian family. It

was held at the home of Speke's brother, a local magistrate, with a jury of local people, and the principal witness was Speke's cousin, supported by a gamekeeper in his employ and a local surgeon. Neither Fuller nor Davis, it appeared, saw the shot fired. Fuller scarcely heard it. The surgeon gave plain, anatomical details, and the jury dutifully returned a verdict of accidental death. The hammer of Speke's gun, suggested the *Times* diplomatically a day or two later, must have "struck against a stone or hitched in a bough."

A squat memorial stone still stands on the site of the tragedy, unsuspected by the passing motorists a hundred yards away and seldom visited by the cottagers across the field ("It's still there so far as I know," as one lady observed to me recently, "if the vandals haven't got it"). And the inscription upon it, at the very spot where the tragedy occurred, boldly admits of no doubt: "Here the distinguished and enterprising African traveller, Captain John Hanning Speke, Lost his life in the accidental explosion of his gun, September 15, 1864."

But kind words butter no parsnips, as they say in Somerset. Is it likely that Speke would shoot himself accidentally? Burton thought not. Writing some years later, he recalled Speke's particular caution with weapons: "I observed that even when our canoe was shaken and upthrown by the hippopotamus he never allowed his gun to look at him or at others." The *Times* thought perhaps overfamiliarity with weapons had bred carelessness, and others suggested that Speke was handier with rifles than he was with shotguns. George Fuller claimed, fifty years later, that both he and the gamekeeper had noticed Speke's lax handling of his gun, which was why they kept well away from him in the field. Still, Speke was always very proud of his gunmanship, and most people thought it odd that after a lifetime's practice he should make so elementary an error as to shoot himself dead by mistake.

Is it likely, then, that Speke would have committed suicide? On the face of it, no. He was a soldier born and bred, nobody denied him courage, and his principles were militantly Christian. With his candid blue eyes, his manly carriage, and his sixth-form appeal, he did not seem the kind to opt out. After all, as the *Chronicle* said in its obituary notice, he was "one of the bravest and most undaunted sons of the noblest nation upon earth."

But his style was deceptive. Like many another gentlemanly son of the noblest nation, he was not entirely what he seemed. He could be spiteful. He was often depressed. If he did not actually lie in his books and letters, he did not always tell the whole truth. Besides, though the Spekes were traditionally soldiers, squires, or clergymen, they had their share of eccentricities: Speke's brother Benjamin, who had taken holy orders, married against his family's wishes, ran away to London, was once arrested as a murder suspect, and for a time vanished altogether, claiming afterward that he had been locked up in a dungeon in the Strand.

Speke was not one of your calm and measured English paragons: he was a man of tormented impulses, suppressed fervors, and unforgiving grudges. Constitutionally he seems, when one gets to know him, quite a likely suicide; circumstantially, it might be thought, he had reason enough to despair.

He was right about the Nile, as we know now, but was he *sure* he was right? Did he have doubts about other sources of the river, was he nervous about the lacunae in his knowledge, which Burton would certainly expose? At moments of stress, as of triumph, Speke habitually expressed himself in bloodshed, if only the controlled bloodshed of a shotgun and a passing bird. Perhaps that subconscious urge to kill, as an outlet for the emotions, went a stage farther that day and became an instinct of self-destruction—something less than a controlled suicide but more than pure accident.

But we shall never know. In the cen-

Speke's tomb lies in the vault of his rural parish church.   Burton's tomb, a marble tent, squats in a London suburb.

tury since that inquest the truth has become still further muffled, for it turned out that George Fuller was so unreliable a witness as to make the inquest evidence meaningless. In two depositions he later contradicted much of what was said that day—about the type of gun Speke was using, about its condition when he found it, about Speke's posture as he crossed the wall, even about the time of death. Speke, Fuller now maintained, had never been to Bath that morning, and certainly had never met Burton, whose reference to their last encounter was "a specimen from the many heroics of Richard Burton, that is characteristic of his vivid imagination." As for the death weapon, it vanished, and has never been found.

Thus we must draw our own conclusions. The facts are few and dubious. All is hazy, blurred in the mist of that afternoon long ago, so that we can only follow the example of John Hanning Speke himself, and honor our instincts.

Burton lived for another twenty-six years. He never went back to Africa, and doubtless regretted to the end of his life the day he allowed Speke to go off to the Northern Lake without him. But he made his fortune with the first unexpurgated translation of *The Arabian Nights,* and after a lifetime of furious controversy, fluctuation, scholarship, and adventure, died famous and a Knight of the Bath—suspect to the end among the orthodox, looking in old

age as magnificently sinister as ever, and idolized still by the faithful, fatuous Isabel, who took the posthumous precaution of burning most of his journals and many unpublished manuscripts.

For his tomb Isabel erected, in the Catholic cemetery of Mortlake, London, an Arab tent made of marble, fitted up as a chapel inside, with real camel bells that tinkled when the door was opened and room for two coffins. It is still there, chipped and forlorn, directly opposite the headquarters of the East Sheen Scout Group. If you stand in Worple Street, while the commuter trains rattle by and the jets scream over to London Airport, you can see its pyramidal mock draperies protruding over the cemetery wall. Isabel has long since been reunited with Richard inside, and on a slab at the sealed door is a poem by Justin Huntly McCarthy:

Oh, last and noblest of the errant knights,
The English soldier and the Arab Shiek [sic],
Oh, Singer of the East who loved so well
The deathless wonder of the Arabian Nights,
Who touched Camoens lute and still would seek
Ever new deeds until the end, farewell.

But Speke is buried with a solider romance. Deep in the green silence of the Somerset countryside, among thatch and apple orchards, stands the church of St. Andrew at Dowlish Wake, in a village still insulated against the traffic of the main roads, unhurried and unperturbed. This is the sanctuary of the Spekes. Spekes are everywhere inside. There are Speke memorial win-

dows. There are Speke commemorative plaques. There is a Speke vault and a Speke chapel. Three Spekes are on the list of rectors, two Spekes served in the First World War, four Spekes died in the Second. Here is a pair of fifteenth-century Spekes, recumbent with weepers near the altar, and here, in brass, is the sixteenth-century Speke *"qui edificavit hanc partem ecclesie."*

At the heart of it all, flanked by a Union Jack brought home from Jinja, John Hanning Speke himself stands in stately, life-size bust, bearded and masterly, above the big black marble sarcophagus containing his remains—ornamented by laurel leaves, embellished with gun, sword, and sextant, and supported, as the College of Heralds decreed, by a Crocodile on the dexter side and a large Hippopotamus sinister.

So Speke won in the end. There are still Spekes about in that countryside, much respected still—"people of the old sort, you know"—and true to his heritage, the explorer is among them. A family man to the last, an English gentleman of the rooted kind, his half-suppressed, half-ashamed romanticism sustains him in death as it impelled him in life. In 1875 Henry Stanley established, once and for all, the truth of that tragic intuition on the shores of the Northern Lake, and since then no one has disputed Speke's right to the proud Latin epitaph upon his tomb: E NILO PRAECLARUS—ILLUSTRIOUS FOR THE NILE.

The Bloodiest Battle in History

It was the Somme in 1916, and there, on the windy downlands of northern France, the "flower" of European manhood was slaughtered. How much else was lost in what F. Scott Fitzgerald called "the last love battle"?

By ROBERT COWLEY

The old Roman road from Albert to Bapaume is twelve miles long and absolutely straight. Even allowing for a token deceleration through the three or four brief villages along the way, with their harsh straggle of brick houses and barns, you can scarcely avoid making the trip in twenty minutes or less. La Boisselle, Pozières, Le Sars: the highway is their main street, and except for an occasional tractor, nothing holds you up.

The beginning of the great plain of northern France is a landscape empty of surprises until you notice the cemeteries. They seem to sprout up everywhere and in the most unlikely places: not only by the side of the road, but out in the middle of a wheat field or in the shadow of a dark and isolated burst of woodland. A faint ground swell may produce hundreds of headstones, a long gully, thousands, close-packed in orderly rows and boxed behind brick walls, like weathered tent cities turned into marble by mistake. The cemeteries give you a start at first, but you are past them soon enough.

More than half a century ago, when the First World War battle of the Somme was fought here in 1916, it was inconceivable that the land could ever again support anything but cemeteries. Five months of massed artillery fire turned these rich plains and gentle downs into a wasteland, "the most terrifying devastated area perhaps ever seen on our planet," the poet Edmund Blunden wrote. Wilfred Owen, who may have been the most talented of the extraordinary group of British writers to serve on the Somme, surveyed the awesome prospect of the battlefield soon after the storm had subsided. He was fresh from England, and the contact must have been unbearable. "It is pock-marked like a body of foulest disease," he told his mother, "and its odour is the breath of cancer."

Everything about the battle of the Somme stupefies: the pulverized landscape, the profligate expenditure of matériel, the astronomical carnage, and not least, the infinitesimal gains made by the greatest and most prolonged offensive that armies had yet attempted. From July until mid-November, 1916, the British ground their way up the road from Albert, a few hundred blasted yards at a time. They never did reach Bapaume that year, though troops shivering in the slimy trenches

and waterlogged shell holes that passed for the ultimate front line could make out the tallest buildings three miles away, their fractured roofs showing above a last, long, tantalizing rise. Nowhere did the British, or their French allies fighting astride the river Somme, drive the German Army back more than seven miles on a front twenty-odd miles long; in places they gained nothing at all. They called it a victory anyway, and perhaps it was by Western Front standards. The debate has never been settled to anyone's real satisfaction.

The debate goes on about the losses, too. Nobody knows exactly how many were killed, wounded, or taken prisoner in those four and a half months: over the years informed estimates have varied by the hundreds of thousands. Three million men fought on the Somme at one time or another; perhaps a third of them became casualties. The figure most widely accepted today is 600,000 *for each side*. If that is not unreasonable, then neither is the estimate of 200,000 to 300,000 dead. "I think 7,000 corpses to the square mile is not much of an exaggeration, ten to the acre shall we say, and your nose told you where they lay thickest," wrote

Next stop, Berlin: On their way to the front, soldiers of the New Armies wave for an official photographer.

Charles Carrington, who was there. All can agree on one point, however: the Somme is the bloodiest battle in history.

Only consider the evidence recorded on the memorial arch at Thiepval. It can be seen for miles, its rusty brick setbacks squatting dourly on the ridge-line. You might mistake it for a factory at first. From a distance, the stone facing around the lower piers looks strangely weathered—but then, as you climb the steps, the weathering resolves into names, thousands upon thousands of them, etched into the graying marble. The names—"these intolerably nameless names," Siegfried Sassoon called them—seem to spurt out of the stone of the graceless central arch, starting at such a height that you have to bend your neck back sharply to make out the topmost ones. The names inundate the walls of the subarchways with the same torrential weight. This is the memorial to the British and Empire dead in the battle of the Somme who have no known grave—in that sinister euphemism of the Great War, "the missing." There are 73,077 names on the Thiepval arch.

If time has made these names more nameless than intolerable, it has not

yet erased the trauma: the Somme, as Correlli Barnett has written, left "a lasting and terrible impression on the British memory." What amount of pain is concealed in the words you see again and again, scrawled in the cemetery registers: "Beautifully kept, as always"? It is hard to grasp how people in places like Accrington and Grimsby must have felt when, in a period of days in July, 1916, they received hundreds of telegrams of condolence. In some working-class towns there were streets from which all the men simply vanished; too often the officers responsible for keeping casualty lists had been swept away with the rest. *The Times* printed sixty-eight columns of names of men killed and wounded in the first four weeks. And even now, every autumn, an old lady arrives in a chauffered Rolls at the Guards Cemetery in Lesboeufs. With ghostly regularity she has returned on the same date, the day her husband was killed here, as if clinging to an old grief like Miss Havisham to her wedding dress.

There is a good deal of truth in the assertion that "the flower of British manhood" fell at the Somme—that the

dead and maimed represented "the heart of a whole generation." The men who went over the top on those chalky downlands were the best the country had to offer, the volunteers of 1914 and 1915 who had swelled, by the hundreds of thousands, the "New Armies" raised by the Secretary of State for War, Lord Kitchener. "Never before," said the Official History of the eve of the Somme, "had the ranks of a British Army on the field of battle contained the finest of all classes of the nation in physique, brains and education."

Recruiting officers had been overwhelmed by men of all ages, rushing to join before it was too late. Schoolboy chums had bicycled over dusty country lanes to regimental depots and had been told to come back when they were older; they had simply gone somewhere else and had falsified their ages. Leeds, Birmingham, and other big towns had raised, sometimes at their own expense, "City" or "Pals" battalions (as they were called in the north of England). So had individual occupations—the 3rd Manchester Pals, for instance, were drawn from the clerks and warehousemen of the city, and the 15th Highland Light Infantry from the Glas-

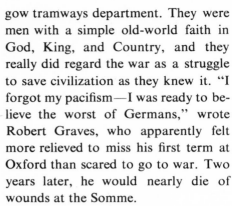

Wilfred Owen

Robert Graves

Siegfried Sassoon

Harold Macmillan

gow tramways department. They were men with a simple old-world faith in God, King, and Country, and they really did regard the war as a struggle to save civilization as they knew it. "I forgot my pacifism—I was ready to believe the worst of Germans," wrote Robert Graves, who apparently felt more relieved to miss his first term at Oxford than scared to go to war. Two years later, he would nearly die of wounds at the Somme.

But then, the heaviest proportion of losses were always among junior officers like Graves—the subalterns who, at that stage of the war, came exclusively from the public schools and universities. These young men of the upper classes were precisely the ones destined to become the next generation of British leaders: the politicians, colonial officials, high civil servants, teachers, writers, and innovators in general. During the months of the Somme, the Roll of Honour in the *Illustrated London News* or the *Sphere,* that social page of the war dead, overflowed with their soft, well-scrubbed, and aristocratic faces. The future military theorist and historian, Basil Liddell Hart, went to France in charge of eight junior officers; he was himself just twenty-one. Five of them died on the first day of the battle, and the rest, including Liddell Hart, were all casualties by the end of July. The front-line officers were usually a head taller than the working-class men they commanded, they were required to go before them in an attack, to set an example, and most of them still wore different, and easily recognizable, uniforms. (Along with so much else, the Somme changed that: subalterns began carrying rifles and dressing like their men.)

One of the appalling things about the Somme is that none of the people responsible were ever sure what they wanted the battle to accomplish. The site of the attack was chosen for political, not strategic, reasons: the British and French armies joined just north of the banks of the Somme River, in the department of the same name, and Mar-

shall Joffre, the French commander in chief, persuaded his British counterpart, Sir Douglas Haig, that the two allies should go on the offensive side by side. Haig was realistic enough to see that the Somme area was of little military importance, as well as being an excessively strong part of the German line, and he would have preferred to strike elsewhere. But apparently the dapper little Lowland Scot, the martial blend in a famous distilling family, tended to be shy in debate.

Then, in February, 1916, the Germans attacked at Verdun, and as the French desperately fed division after division into that notorious sausage grinder, a collapse seemed near if some sort of diversion was not soon mounted: *faute de mieux,* preparations for the Somme went on. As if carried away by the heady immensity of his own operation, Haig became convinced that a breakout was possible after all. He spoke hopefully of sending his cavalry through the ruptured German line, and of reaching Bapaume and the open country beyond in the first days of July.

"You must know that I feel that every step in my plan has been taken with the Divine help," he wrote to his wife on June 30, the eve of the Big Push. Haig was by no means alone in his trust in the Almighty. That night a young subaltern named J. S. Engall was confiding similar thoughts to his parents. He described a communion service that he had attended with many of his comrades, and added: "I have a strong feeling that I shall come through safely; nevertheless should it be God's holy will to call me away, I am quite prepared to go. . . . I could not wish for a finer death . . ."

His letter must have reached home

at about the same time as the telegram from the War Office. Engall was one of the twenty thousand Englishmen who died the next day, a day that has been called the most disastrous in the history of British arms since Hastings.

You signed on to die—we all recognized that," said the old colonel who was my landlord in London, one night shortly before I went to the Somme. "But then, there is no greater thrill in life than to come close to losing it." He only talked to me about the war that once, and I wonder if he really supposed that someone my age would understand. A contemporary of his recently wrote that "it seemed that the only real life was to be found where there was the greatest chance of meeting death." Such sentiments do not go over easily in the era of Vietnam, and yet the reasoning came naturally to that generation. How else do you explain the events of July 1? The day could happen not only because of what men expected of themselves but because of what they had allowed their leaders to expect of them.

They were so young, the dead of the Somme, and their youth is almost more painful to contemplate than their numbers. An oblique reference in this memoir, a passing mention in that biography, give you an idea of who they were—or of what they might have become. "I went down to Oxford," writes Julian Huxley, "and was offered a fellowship in Zoology at New College; I was taking the place of my erstwhile tutor, Geoffrey Smith, whose brilliant career was cut short when he was killed on the Somme." Here is Harold Macmillan, remembering his friend Edward Tennant ("Bimbo" to all), killed in

Raymond Asquith

Edmund Blunden

H. H. Munro (Saki)

Basil Liddell Hart

September at the age of nineteen: "Born of talented parents, he seemed to illustrate in his person all the Elizabethan ardour that still gave some enchantment and excitement to war." ("Poor jester Bim," Lady Cynthia Asquith lamented.) Or listen to the poet Siegfried Sassoon, talking about a fellow officer from Cambridge, whose specialty was the history of Roman Britain: ". . . there was an expression of veiled melancholy on his face, as if he were inwardly warned that he would never see his home in Wiltshire again. A couple of months afterwards I saw his name in one of the long lists of the killed."

The true lost generation of Sassoon's time lies under those fields. You could pick any of the cemeteries of the Somme and arrive at the same conclusion, but the one I particularly remember is the cemetery of the Devonshire Regiment, near Fricourt. It is small as these places go, merely two longish rows of headstones at the top of a steep and wooded bank. Everybody in it (except for one 1918 burial) died on July 1, 1916.

The headstones are the same as those in all the British cemeteries. They are like sections of marble plank, endlessly sawed off at regular intervals, with the regimental seal carved above the pertinent information—name, rank, serial number, date of death, and age. Often you find just the words: "A Soldier of the Great War" or "A Soldier of the Devonshire Regiment." At the base of many of the headstones, but half-obscured by flowers and ornamental bushes, are short inscriptions that the (then) Imperial War Graves Commission permitted widows or families to select. Here, as in the other cemeteries, the inscriptions seldom vary, and in the aggregate they have an unexpected power—homely sentiments that, like the Great War itself, better belong to the nineteenth century than to the twentieth: "In Loving Memory/ Anchored Safe/Where Storms are Over" (11255 Private William Browning/Devonshire Rgt./1st July 1916/ Age 19) . . . "Until the Day Dawns" (Age 18) . . . "His Time was Short" (Age 20). Occasionally there is a hint less of a heavenly future than of a promising past cut short in the little valley below: "Late of the Malay States/Elder Son/Of Gerald Davidson/Suez, Egypt" (Age 31). The mark of the Empire is stamped all over this place.

On July 1 the Devonshires had gone down this bank by the hundreds, one long line plodding after another. Their orders required them to advance at an even walking pace, but they could not have moved much faster if they had wanted to. Each one carried "fighting order" weighing at least sixty-six pounds. This included their rifles, steel helmets, trench shovels, wire cutters, water bottles, rolled groundsheets, haversacks (containing mess tins, towels, shaving kits, iodine, field dressings, extra cheese, and extra socks), two gas helmets and tear goggles, two bandoleers of small arms ammunition, two Mills grenades, and two sandbags. Sixty-six pounds was more than half the average weight of the British soldier in 1916; an Army mule was not expected to carry more than a third of its weight. But it was thought that they would need these things on the other side.

Like everyone else that morning, the Devonshires came under fire immediately from a machine gun across the valley. Scores were hit. Was Private 11255 Anchored Safe in those first moments, I wonder, or did he find his Shelter from Earthly Storms on the German wire below? ("I've seen 'em, I've seen 'em," the song went. "Hanging on the old barbed wire.") Did the Day begin to Dawn for A Soldier of the Great War in the obliterating explosion of a whiz-bang where the railroad tracks once ran below?

Summer days as perfect as July 1, 1916, are extraordinary in that part of the world. Everyone who survived remembered the blue, cloudless sky and the broiling sun. As he looked on from a support trench, Sassoon penciled an entry in his notebook: "I am staring at a sunlit picture of Hell . . ." Six British corps, thirteen divisions, or 140,000 infantry, went over the top that morning. The British had fired 1,627,824 shells in the seven days leading up to Z Day. It only remained for the infantry to walk over. But the damage too often proved to be only cosmetic. No one, apparently, suspected the extent to which the Germans had honeycombed the chalk soil of the Somme ridges with deep dugouts, most of them impervious to even the heaviest shells. Some were tunneled as much as thirty or forty feet below the long, gray grass and the ever-present poppies, and were equipped with bunks and electric lights; a few of the officers' quarters had paneled walls decorated with cretonne. When the shelling started, the German front-line garrisons crowded into these claustrophobic shafts, short of food and space, assaulted by lyddite fumes and the seismic din overhead, but otherwise safe. The moment the barrage lifted, they were ready to dash up and run to the nearest shell crater, dragging machine guns and ammunition boxes with them.

If both sides literally found themselves racing against death, one intervening presence gave the Germans the edge they needed. That was their barbed wire. Like metallic hedgerows, belts of

CREDITS: WILFRED OWEN, EDMUND BLUNDEN: IMPERIAL WAR MUSEUM; ROBERT GRAVES, SIEGFRIED SASSOON, RAYMOND ASQUITH, H. H. MUNRO: MANSELL COLL.; HAROLD MACMILLAN: COURTESY OF RICHARD GARNETT, ESQ., MACMILLAN CO., LTD., LONDON; BASIL LIDDELL HART: COURTESY CASSELL & CO., LTD., LONDON.

it stretched for mile after unbroken mile, hanging in festoons from post to post or simply lying in piles, as much as forty yards wide in places. One variety had barbs as thick as a man's thumb. "It was so dense," a British private remembered, "that daylight could barely be seen through it. Through the glasses it looked like a black mass."

But the British showed a gift for creating their own obstacles, and the time of the attack, 7:30 A.M., was one of them. By then the sun was already high and there was neither semidarkness nor morning haze to confound the view of the enemy gunners. The French had insisted—and once again Haig had backed down—that the attack be made in full daylight, to allow the artillery a final opportunity to check its effectiveness. The "bewildering tumult" of those last minutes "seemed to grow more insistent with the growing brilliance of the atmosphere and the intenser blue of the July sky." The writer was R. H. Tawney, in years to come a prophet of a socialist England and a major economic thinker, but that morning an anonymous NCO of the Manchester Pals, crouching by a trench ladder somewhere in the same valley that the Devonshires had to cross.

"It was not a succession of explosions or a continuous roar," he said. "It was not a noise; it was a symphony." Others would speak of the same orchestral grandeur of the guns—which swelled to a finale with the kettledrum-like detonation of eleven underground mines, heaving earth and shattered bodies hundreds of feet in the air. To a young Australian officer, Adrian Stephen, watching from an artillery observation post ten miles to the north of Tawney, that "jerky roar . . . flung from horizon to horizon" was "wonderful music—the mightiest I have ever heard. . . . One felt inclined to laugh with the fierce exhilaration of it. After all, it was our voice, the voice of a whole Empire at war."

Then, abruptly, the imperial music stopped. Whistles blew up and down the line, sixteen miles of whistles blow-

ing, with an occasional blast from a hunting horn. Subalterns leaped up on the parapets, gesturing to the men in the packed trenches to follow. Some Highland infantrymen went forward to the skirl of bagpipes, while two companies of Northumberland Fusiliers plodded under the arching path of a rugby ball, drop-kicked, the Official History recorded, "by an eminent North Country player." Like an apparition from another century, one battalion advanced to the beat of a single big drum. But for the most part, bravado of this sort was the stuff of the illustrated weeklies. "They got going without delay," an officer in an Ulster battalion said, "no fuss, no shouting, no running, everything solid and thorough—just like the men themselves. Here and there a boy would wave his hand to me as I shouted good luck to them through my megaphone. And all had a cheery face. Most were carrying loads. Fancy advancing against heavy fire with a big roll of barbed wire on your shoulders."

You would like to freeze the picture forever at this instant: the companies that had crept out in advance of zero time rising (with what effort) from the mustard and the dew-laden grass; the NCO's shouting to the men filing through the gaps in their wire to form up—"Don't bunch. . . . Keep up up on the left"; the bent brown figures moving with a deliberate lack of urgency, generally uphill and everywhere in the open, cocked rifles slung over their right shoulders; the untarnished bayonets of the New Armies flashing in the morning sun; the hares starting at their feet; the smoke candles belching opaque columns, white, green, and orange, and Scots in hodden-gray kilts disappearing into the vapors; the football of the Northumberlands reaching the apex of its flight.

That moment was, as it was meant to be, a consummation. So much was involved in it, so much was at stake—the treasure of Empire and of youth, the sureties of the past, the hopes of the fu-

ture, but not least, the illusions of the present. "The first line appeared to continue without end to right and left. It was quickly followed by a second, then a third and fourth. They came on at a steady, easy pace as if"—the onlooker was a German officer waiting with his men in the shell craters opposite—"as if expecting to find nothing alive in our trenches."

Already the picture is marred in close-up. Men slip down the ladders, dead before they hit the bottom of the trench, or crumble in piles, blocking the narrow passages cut through their own wire. Others, moving across the open to the jumping-off place, never reach their own front line. A whiz-bang clips a sergeant in the throat and his head disappears. A bullet deflates a bagpipe. The rugby ball goes bouncing off, the men behind it "held up," the Official History reports, "by a continuous hail of bullets not far from their front trenches. . . . whole lines . . . were swept down dead or wounded at every further attempt to get forward by rushes." German batteries, untouched by the bombardment, catch jammed assembly trenches just before zero, the cones of the explosions giving the impression of a thick belt of poplar trees.

For the first and probably last time at the Somme, machine guns, not artillery, apparently did more killing. Their methodical work had an unreal, almost epic quality, sweeping away thousands as effortlessly as a storyteller's scythe in a *Ramayana* battle. Men fell, toppled in windrows like cornstalks, often before they had crossed the first hundred yards of No Man's Land; later, burial parties would collect long lines of corpses immediately in front of the British wire.

The Germans had cleverly positioned their trenches along the crest of the ridge where the great plain falls away, leaving the British with few footholds on the high ground when the battle began. Machine guns kept them from exploiting the ones they had. Near Thiepval, a village that the Germans had turned into a fortress, an Ulster officer named Crozier glanced through the trees (or what was left of them) on his way forward: ". . . my eyes are riveted on a sight I shall never see again. It is the 32nd Division at its best. I see rows upon rows of British soldiers lying dead, dying or wounded, in No Man's Land. Here and there I see an officer urging on his followers. Occasionally I can see the hands thrown up and then a body flops on the ground . . ." Crozier and his men had been held in reserve; it was now 8 A.M., and according to the timetable, Thiepval should have fallen fifteen minutes before. He soon learned what had gone wrong. "Again I look southward from a different angle and perceive heaped up masses of British corpses suspended on the German wire, while live men rush forward in orderly procession to swell the weight of numbers in the spider's web. . . . Thiepval village is masked with a wall of corpses."

Attackers snagged kilts or equipment on the wire, tore their clothes off to get free of it, or ran back and forth looking for openings until gunned down. The Somme wire would become tangled in the memory of one generation of Englishmen, civilian soldiers who would promise themselves, with such lamentable consequences for the next, Never Again!

An hour passed. By now the smoke candles had burned out, disclosing a scene of eerie emptiness. Charles Carrington, a schoolboy-turned-subaltern, scanned his bit of front for signs of progress, hopeful or otherwise: though the landscape "must have contained 10,000 men, no one could be seen," he wrote. For a while yet, the high grass would keep the secret of the morning. Some 20,000 men had been killed outright or would die of wounds: 19,240 is the official figure for July 1, and that may err on the conservative side. I have heard that 23,000 or 24,000 may be a truer estimate. The total British losses approached 60,000—two casualties for every yard of front. But after a point the arithmetic of oblivion

becomes meaningless—and in any event, something *was* settled. Along the southern half of the attack, the Allies did push their way up the Somme ridges, and that was success enough for the generals.

Two years in the making and ten minutes in the destroying": the epitaph that one writer bestowed on the New Armies hardly exaggerated. Perhaps something else was destroyed with them. F. Scott Fitzgerald once said of the Great War that "this took religion and years of plenty and tremendous sureties and the exact relation that existed between the classes. . . . You had to have a whole-souled sentimental equipment going back further than you could remember." The spontaneous growth of the New Armies could only have happened because of that past. I can't help thinking that the men who came through July 1 had crossed the divide from one era to another, our own, as boldly and as blindly as they would have negotiated any historical No Man's Land. Could they, or the drafts that succeeded them, be blamed if their faith in God, King, and Country stood up imperfectly to the machine gun and the high-explosive shell?

On the evening of July 2 Haig estimated that his total casualties were "over 40,000 to date." But, he congratulated himself in his diary, "This cannot be considered severe in view of the numbers engaged." Doubtless the lack of solid information reaching him contributed to his early optimism. Closer to the front, however, where the true extent of the disaster was appreciated, a mood of incapacitating depression took hold of corps and division commands. For the next few days the British were mainly content to rest on the small successes of July 1, or to reinforce its failures. They allowed woods and support trenches hastily vacated by the Germans to remain unoccupied—and soon the Germans returned, in force. They sent unenthusiastic battalions over ground already strewn with corpses—and soon there

were a few hundred more of England's flower rotting in the sun.

Attrition became the announced justification for continuing the stalled offensive. If the enemy were bled white enough, the reasoning went, he would eventually have to give in. Attrition, which we have come to think of in terms of the body count, is an inspiration peculiar to this century. Sometimes, however, an uneasy question arises: just who was attriting whom? This may explain why the British official historians took such pains to prove that the Germans had lost more men than the Allies at the Somme. "Of course they didn't want their casualties to be greater than those of the Germans," an archivist at the Imperial War Museum in London told me. "That would have made it a defeat, wouldn't it?"

The war entered a new phase after July 1. "From then onward things hardened into a more relentless, mechanized affair, took on a more sinister aspect," wrote the poet David Jones, who fought with one of the Welsh regiments. The Somme was, as a German military historian put it, "the first material-battle of the World War" — and in the material respect, the British would have, finally, the edge. The fighting crept up the ridges flanking the Roman road and spilled over onto that plain that seems so high, though it is never more than 500-odd feet above sea level. The woods that lie scattered along the edge of the plain seemed to magnetize the action now. Mametz, Trônes, Delville, High Wood—the British became as obsessed with taking them as the Germans did with holding them. In more peaceful times, local men of property had mainly kept them as private hunting preserves; they still do. Two years of neglect had turned these places into formidable obstacles. "To talk of a wood is to talk rot," one British officer said of a leafy objective he had been ordered to secure at all costs. "It was the most dreadful tangle of dense trees and undergrowth imaginable, with deep yawning broken trenches criss-crossing about it; every

Underground war: At La Boisselle on July 1, 1916, an explosive charge at the end of a tunnel left a crater 90 feet deep in the German front line.

tree broken off at top or bottom and branches cut away, so that the floor ... was almost an impossible tangle of timber, trenches, undergrowth, etc., blown to pieces by British and German heavy guns for a week."

Mametz Wood was probably the most famous, partly because persons such as Gerald Brennan and Liddell Hart happened through, and partly because other notable talents such as Graves, Jones, and Sassoon had, by chance or by background, found their way into the Welsh regiments that took most of Mametz. The Welsh went into the wood at dawn on July 10. Let us follow the action of the next twenty-four hours through the eyes and ears of one soldier, Private John Ball, the protagonist of *In Parenthesis*, David Jones's long narrative poem. The day begins with the men rising "dry mouthed from the chalk" and moving up a shorelike incline, wave after diminishing wave, toward the dark wood. A bewildered half-dozen bunch, "like sheep where the wall is tumbled," at a spot where artillery has blasted a passage, and are picked off by Brandenburgers perched in the trees. Ball trips on German wire camouflaged in the undergrowth. All sense of order vanishes. The survivors are engulfed by a "denseness of hazel-brush and body high bramble." The struggle for the wood becomes a confusion of bombs winged above thornbushes, of gray figures withdrawing into further thickets, and of the ominous clank of a machine-gun tripod; of coming into a clearing to find newly-dead comrades "distin-

guished only in their variant mutilation"; of stragglers gathering and falling back and trying vainly to dig in ("But it's no good you can't do it with these toy spades"); of the man next to you hit and dying in your arms ("And get back to that digging can't yer—this ain't a bloody wake"); of trees crashing on wounded men; and of water parties arriving at last with half their bottles punctured.

Night falls: barrage mingles with deafening counterbarrage, and platoons grope forward through the "mazy charnel-ways" of this nightmare wood, seeking "to distinguish men from walking trees and branchy moving like a Birnam copse." Men panic. In the light of a flare, Ball glimpses the severed head of a friend, grinning "like the Cheshire cat." In the early morning hours he, too, is hit in the legs and manages to crawl back to safety: "To groves always men come both to their joy and their undoing."

Robert Graves picked his way through the rubble of corpses in Mametz Wood one chilly July evening, while searching for German overcoats to use as blankets. He came across two men who had "succeeded in bayoneting each other simultaneously"— an unforgettable pair—and were sustained in an upright position by the tree trunk against which they had fallen. Graves collected the overcoats; still feeling superstitious about taking from the dead, he told himself that they were only a loan. But the conventional barriers between living and dead were,

in fact, disappearing. The living cadged food and water and collected souvenirs from the dead, joked about them and slept next to them, and built up their parapets with them when sandbags ran out. The two came to have a kind of ecological interdependence, like that of the Laplander and the reindeer. Once death ceased to be essentially tragic, a whole underpinning of life and literature gave way. Heroes died for no reason—if, indeed, there were heroes left.

But we cannot leave Mametz Wood without mentioning one further item in its catalogue of horrors: poison gas. On the night of July 17–18 the Germans fired gas shells filled with lethal phosgene for the first time, instead of the usual chlorine gas released from stationary cylinders. The only gas shells until then had been the lachrymatory kind that smelled of strong onions: the standing order was not to bother about gas masks, and that night Graves's company, moving up from Mametz Wood, lost half a dozen men.

At about the same time, Basil Liddell Hart was leading his company of Yorkshiremen through the wood in the opposite direction. "We suddenly heard a lot of shells landing around us, but as they did not explode with a bang, we imagined that they must be duds— until there was a strong smell of gas.... Coughing violently, I stayed to warn and divert the platoons that were following." The next morning he was sent back on a stretcher, "feeling bad, but still unaware how bad." The tall, thin subaltern had been a runner in school, and his strong lungs probably saved his life. His war was over, but the most influential military historian of our time would spend the rest of his life elaborating on the original lessons of the Somme. In eighteen days he had seen enough of generals who bungled and missed chances by what he called the rigidity of their own inertia: his ideas would not be lost on other generations of military leaders, whether they were Nazis blitzkrieging through France and Russia or the Israelis who twice burst across the Sinai.

By the middle of the month the British confronted not only the German second fixed line of defense but the problem of how to avoid a repetition of the July 1 slaughter when they stormed it. This time they tried something new, surprise. In the darkness after midnight on July 14, lines of men inched wormlike up the slopes, following white tapes laid down earlier in No Man's Land, and assembled as close to the enemy wire as they could get without risking discovery. For once the British had not tipped their hand with a prolonged bombardment. At 3:20 A.M., just as the sky was beginning to pale, the artillery opened fire. Five minutes later the infantry went forward. It breached a three-and-a-half-mile gap in the enemy's last completed trench system before the morning was over, and established a secure foothold along the crest of the ridge.

Liddell Hart, who came up afterward, was treated to the unaccustomed spectacle of gray-clad corpses outnumbering khaki ones. Some twenty-two thousand English troops had taken part, hardly more than the number who had died on July 1. Something rare in the experience of the Western Front happened that day. Open country, untouched by fighting, beckoned. Patrols, and even a careless brigadier, ventured far out into the wheat and barley, growing wild now, and saw nothing but a few horse-drawn guns and limbers disappearing, pell-mell, to the rear. High Wood, a seventy-five-acre copse that managed to dominate the plateau from its slight eminence, lay empty.

But the infantry, according to plan, stopped to wait for the cavalry. The cavalry did not appear until just before 7 P.M. After a day of rain showers the sky was clearing, and the wide fields were flooded with that haunting amber light of midsummer evenings in northern France, faintly chilly yet almost Mediterranean. Two squadrons advanced, pennants fluttering, bugles blowing, lances spearing an occasional fugitive hidden in the ripening grain. It was a scene as memorable as it was meaningless. By 9:30, when darkness made further mounted action impracticable, the horsemen drew up in the shelter of a convenient road bank. They had advanced less than a mile, and they were withdrawn that night. Meanwhile, two battalions of infantry had finally penetrated High Wood, but were held up by the undergrowth, a few Germans, the magnifying shadows, and their own inanition. High Wood—or what was left of it—would not fall for another two months.

Like the sepia-toned photographs of the Big Push that appeared week after week in the *Illustrated London News*, there is an unreal quality, monochromatic and at times out of focus, to events during the rest of the summer. The British attacked, the Germans counterattacked: little of value was gained, little was lost. British casualties settled down to a norm of 2,500 per day, and the Germans probably suffered about the same number. That ominous phrase, "at all costs," seemed to creep into the official language of both sides in direct proportion to diminishing results. As the German Supreme Commander, General Erich von Falkenhayn, announced, "The enemy must not be allowed to advance except over corpses."

"At all costs": Both high commands made particularly liberal use of the words at Delville Wood, which earned a reputation as the worst battle-hell of the Somme. The "Devil's Wood" became an inferno. Smoke and gases formed a canopy impervious to light, and trees continued to burn in spite of heavy rains. Those 154 acres consumed six German divisions. A South African survivor spoke of seeing the earth "strewn every yard with the rags of human bodies." Today, only one stump of the original wood remains, wedged like a piece of Tasso's oak between two intertwining trunks.

"At all costs": In July and August, the Australians purchased, for a price of twenty-three thousand men, a mile square of crater fields around the village of Pozières—high, even by the going rate. Everyone speaks of the shellfire. Frank Richards, who served as a private in the Welsh Fusiliers, and who later wrote an extraordinary memoir of the war out of boredom with life on the dole, describes a scene of death warmed over that sounds like a black satire of war. Richards and his company were holding a shallow trench running through a village cemetery near High Wood when a German barrage caught them: "In the cemetery the shells were throwing corpses and coffins clean out of the graves, and some of our killed were now lying alongside of them. We could only sit tight and grin and bear it. One shell burst just outside the trench not far from me, and a man had one side of his face cut clean away by a piece of shell. He was also hit low down but was still conscious. His two pals were deliberating whether they would put him out of his misery or not; fortunately they were spared that, as he died before they had made up their minds. One of our old stretcher-bearers went mad and started to undress himself. He was uttering horrible screams, and we had to fight with him and overpower him . . ."

"At all costs": At the end of July Haig wrote in his diary that "Our losses in July's fighting totalled about 120,000 more than they would have been had we not attacked. They cannot be regarded as sufficient to justify any anxiety as to our ability to continue the offensive." One of the most chilling things about the Somme is that basically decent men could regard these figures so dispassionately. But their apparent indifference may have been no more than a reflection of the chasm then existing between leaders and led. Their backgrounds, predominantly upper class and strenuously insulated from the masses they would command, had hardly prepared them to act in any other way. The Great War generals were the same persons who thought that £75 a year was a proper wage for a working man and whose only sight of the East End slums was from the window of an express speeding out of Liverpool Street. The gap would narrow in the Second World War, largely because the men who became its generals had themselves endured the democratizing miseries of the trenches as young captains and majors. "Indeed, of all the war," a young Guards officer admitted to his mother, "I think the most interesting (and humbling too) experience is the knowledge one gets of the poorer classes." The writer was a future Prime Minister, Harold Macmillan.

The Somme had gotten so far out of control that at times it assumed the character less of battle than of natural disaster. Nothing, apparently, not even the introduction of a possibly decisive secret weapon, could alter the inevitability of stalemate. The secret weapon was the tank. Though the idea of a heavily-armored vehicle running on caterpillar treads had been discussed for several years, it took the initiative of Winston Churchill, as First Lord of the Admiralty, to order the earliest working model of a "land battleship." Early in 1915 he illegally allotted some £70,000 of Admiralty funds for the experiment. When he was forced to resign that spring as a result of the Gallipoli fiasco, he convinced his successor, Arthur Balfour, not to scrap it. A single prototype, christened the H.M.S. *Centipede,* gave a secret performance before a select audience of Cabinet ministers and War Office and GHQ

representatives in February, 1916. David Lloyd George, then Minister of Munitions, watched the "ungainly monster," trapezoid-shaped and splendidly ponderous, "plough through thick entanglements, wallow through deep mud, and heave its huge bulk over parapets and various trenches. . . . Mr. Balfour's delight was as great as my own, and it was only with difficulty that some of us persuaded him to disembark from H.M. Landship while she crossed the last test, a trench several feet wide."

The boyish enthusiasm of the politicians was catching, and the Army ordered a hundred of the tanks. The Mark I tank was big enough to carry a hot and uncomfortable crew of one officer and seven men. Its maximum speed was 3.7 mph and it got one-half mile to the gallon. Two heavy wheels connected to the back provided an additional aid to steering. Much to the consternation of Churchill, who warned of exposing the secret prematurely, Haig determined to use tanks in a third all-out attempt to crack the German line, this time on September 15. The general appeared more eager to redeem the fading prospects of his offensive than to give the tank a fair trial. Crews were scarcely trained and had only the sketchiest of tactical guidelines to follow; some of the delicate behemoths were already worn out from long hours on the proving grounds.

Instead of concentrating the machines in the hope of a single, shattering breakout—the "expanding torrent" principle that Liddell Hart would preach with such effect—Haig allowed them to be parceled out in "packets" scattered along a ten-mile front. In some places the tanks went ahead of the infantry, clearing the way, in others they crawled at a respectful distance behind it, mopping up, accompanied by an officer and six men who moved the wounded from their path. Tanks broke down immediately, split their treads, got stuck in the crater fields or hung up astride German trenches, lost direction and fired on their own men,

Zero time, Z Day: At 7:30 A.M. on July 1, 1916, a motion-picture camera records the first moments of the Big Push. From top to bottom, opposite, troops crouch in a shallow assault trench, then follow an officer over the top. In the third picture, a man (far right) is hit as he stands up, and slides back into the deserted trench, dead.

obeyed confused orders to turn back, or cruised around killing aimlessly until hit and disabled. (Their operative speed turned out to be 1/2 mph, making them choice targets.) A few Germans even panicked at the sight of them and ran or surrendered. Harold Macmillan noted "one or two of these strange objects moving about, and one definitely bogged down in a huge shellhole. They were useful, but not decisive," he concluded after the debut of the dominant weapon of land warfare in the twentieth century. Macmillan himself was wounded in the thigh and pelvis while trying to silence a machine gun. He managed to roll down into a crater, where he lay for twelve hours, pretending to be dead when German counterattackers surged around the lip. In his pocket he carried a copy of Aeschylus's *Prometheus* in Greek, which he read intermittently. "It was a play I knew very well, and seemed not inappropriate to my position." That was the way it was with the educated elite of Macmillan's generation, and their cultivated chutzpah would often seem worth a multitude of faults later on. He nearly died of his wounds.

But useless though the secret weapon may have been, it provided the press with an incident. Toward 8:30 A.M. a reconnaissance plane reported sighting a tank "with large numbers of British troops following it" through the main street of Flers, a village a mile and a half behind the German front line. Correspondents hungering for a bone of good news fleshed out this information with a meaty detail—the troops were cheering. This was what caught the imagination at home, and it provided Haig with the public-relations triumph that had eluded him all sum-

CONTINUED ON PAGE 116

"Shockingly Mad, Madder Than Ever, Quite Mad!"

So said Horace Walpole about a painting by Henry Fuseli. But the young Romantic Age had a penchant for madness; hence all the mad scenes that marked its artists' revolt against reason

The art of the preceding epoch had celebrated the Great and the Beautiful; it was an age of equestrian statues and of paintings of gentlewomen being serenaded in pleasure gardens. But then, almost as though the French Revolution had given the starting signal for this kind of terror as well, the rococo dream dissolves into the romantic nightmare, and the arts proceed to disgorge all the suppressed fears and ferocities of the human imagination. Now it is not field marshals on horseback but demons of lust who ride wildcats and broomsticks in Goya's *Caprichos;* the only beautiful women are the ones being sold by hideous whoremongers, and the myth of a polite, perfectible society is transformed into repulsive images.

Here, a century before Freud, Goya provides the illustrations for a jungle book of the psychopathic subconscious. In the *capricho* entitled *The Sleep of Reason Produces Monsters* (right) he even shows us how it was done: a portrait of the artist as a young dreamer, haunted by the phantoms that have

The Sleep of Reason Produces Monsters is Goya's title for this engraving, one of the famous Caprichos *series, published in 1799. Mad Kate (opposite), the melodramatic study of a demented woman, is the work of Henry Fuseli, the Swiss painter who transplanted himself to London in the 1760's and became part of the English romantic movement. Kate is an illustration for a poem by William Cowper (himself intermittently mad), which features her as the village lunatic, driven out of her wits by the death of her lover. Fuseli shows her crouching on a rock, hair and dress aswirl—an apt symbol of the mad underworld of European romanticism.*

sprung from his own overheated brain. We know that Goya had firsthand knowledge of the sleep of reason, for he went to the madhouse of Saragossa to study scenes of demonic possession among the violently insane. The result is a typically ambiguous painting known as *The Madhouse* (page 81), in which the half-naked lunatics perform their antics before black-robed visitors who seem, on closer inspection, to be rather more sinister than the inmates.

Goya is a very Spanish painter, but these were not merely local lunacies, escaped from an asylum where the Inquisition still held sway and madness was regarded as a kind of *lèse-majesté* against God. Throughout Europe there were young romantics who were as fascinated by the irrational as their fathers had been by the promise that reason would solve everything. The French Revolution, originally advertised as the culmination of the age of reason, had served to destroy both the old order and the belief that intellect could be elevated to take its place. Now it was the emotions' turn to be consulted

By FREDERIC V. GRUNFELD

about the future of mankind. Hence the cult of feeling that arrives with the romantic quest for new forms of art and society. Passion is at a premium. Poetry, says Wordsworth in his preface to the *Lyrical Ballads,* represents "the spontaneous overflow of powerful feelings." For Keats, all human passions are, like love, "creative of essential beauty." Blake says that "Exuberance is Beauty," and as usual goes straight to the heart of the matter: "Sooner murder an infant in its cradle than nurse unacted desires."

Like Goya, Blake felt a special affinity for the creatures of the mental underworld. His engraving of *The Madhouse* presents a compassionate view of that dreaded London institution, Bedlam (originally Bethlehem Hospital), where—as he says in his great poetic vision of Jerusalem—men have built "Dens of despair in the house of bread" (Bethlehem means "house of bread" in Hebrew).

His friend Henry Fuseli did a drawing of a still more theatrical madhouse episode showing a lunatic trying to escape from his warders. Based on "a real scene in the Hospital of S. Spirito at Rome," it was supposed to depict a certain psychological type whose favorite subjects are said to be "Spectres, Demons, and madmen; fantoms, exterminating angels; murders and acts of violence." This description could very well apply to Fuseli himself and his penchant for drawing the macabre: an old man watching a young girl imprisoned with a skeleton, a beautiful woman arranging her hair as the executioner, with his axe at the ready, looks on, an incubus squatting on a sleeping girl's chest while a nightmare sticks her fell head through the bed curtains.

His painting of *The Mandrake,* now lost, struck the aging Horace Walpole as "shockingly mad, madder than ever, quite mad!" but Fuseli would hardly have regarded that as an insult. Much of the time he was trading on madness the way lesser painters exploited sunsets. For his Shakespeare illustrations he painted, among others, the mad Lady Macbeth and Lear raging on the heath; from Milton's *Paradise Lost,* to justify still another madhouse scene, he chose the vision of the lazar house (Book XI) whose inmates suffer from "Daemoniac Phrenzie, moaping Melancholie/And Moon-struck madness, pining Atrophie . . ."

The way to the asylum thus becomes a pilgrimage for artists with sketchbooks under their arms. In the 1820's Géricault, the first of the great French romantic painters, set up his easel in the Salpêtrière Hospital in Paris to do a series of ten portraits of mental patients. The idea had been suggested to him by a young psychiatrist, Dr. Georget, whose book *De la Folie* had made him an authority on madness at twenty-five; Géricault intended to record the particular facial expressions associated with various types of madness—kleptomania, hysteria, criminal compulsion, and so on. Géricault's friend Delacroix followed his example and produced two historical paintings of *Tasso in the Madhouse* (see opposite). Both show the great sixteenth-century poet lost in schizoid reveries, ignoring the taunts of his fellow inmates.

It is no coincidence that Delacroix's

MUSÉE DES BEAUX-ARTS, GHENT—SCALA

Titled Mad Murderer, *or sometimes* Kleptomaniac, *this is the portrait of an inmate of a Paris asylum painted in the 1820's by Théodore Géricault, who was among the first artists to become interested in the theme of madness.*

Tasso bears a marked resemblance to the traditional "Christ Mocked by Soldiers." To the romantics Tasso was a Christlike culture hero, a poet who went mad for the sake of his art. One of the earliest German romantics, Wilhelm Heinse, was the first to write about Tasso as the exemplary madman who had fallen victim to the world's conspiracy against love and genius. Then Goethe took up the theme, to write one of his finest dramas about him; Liszt composed a piano piece and two symphonic tone poems; Donizetti a three-act opera. Lord Byron, in *The Lament of Tasso,* has the poet falsely imprisoned for imputed insanity in an asylum where he is made to suffer "Sickness of heart, and narrowness of place":

Where laughter is not mirth, nor thought
    the mind,
Nor words a language, nor ev'n men man-
    kind;
Where cries reply to curses, shrieks to
    blows,
And each is tortured in his separate
    hell—
For we are crowded in our solitudes—
Many, but each divided by the wall,
Which echoes Madness in her babbling
    moods . . .

Though he claims to have been sane when he came, he feels himself slowly going mad "From long infection of a den like this,/Where the mind rots congenial with the abyss . . ."

None of this has much to do with the actual life of Tasso, who was confined by the Duke of Ferrara for the defensible reason that he was insane and had to be kept out of the way of the Inquisition. But the function of the romantic artist-madman is literary, not historical; he provides access to the long-neglected darker sides of passion and imagination and helps to demolish the eighteenth-century convention that man is subject to the rule of reason.

Madness makes all symbols possible, and the sleep of reason is one of the ways a writer can probe and expand the limits of his domain. Goethe's Faust is the exemplary neurotic of the age ("Two souls live, *Ach!* within my breast . . ."), and Gretchen goes completely mad; together, with the help of their therapist, Mephistopheles, they break through to deeper psychological levels than any characters since Shakespeare's. It was Shakespeare, incidentally, who taught the romantic playwrights how sweet are the uses of insanity in the theatre ("The lunatic, the lover, and the poet/Are of imagination all compact . . ."). The great mad scenes in works like *Faust* and *Lucia di Lammermoor*—the frenzied laugh, the disheveled hair, the plaintive ditty sung by witless maid—all derive in one way or another from Ophelia, Lear, or Lady Macbeth.

These are symptoms of a literary dementia that takes a tremendous toll among Bellini's and Donizetti's heroines. For a clinical description of a typical case we need look no farther than Sir Walter Scott's *Bride of Lammermoor,* the novel on which Donizetti's *Lucia* is based. The story comes to a climax after Lucy has stabbed her rejected bridegroom on their wedding night and her parents find her in the chimney corner of the bridal chamber,

seated, or rather crouched like a hare upon its form—her head-gear dishevelled; her night-clothes torn and dabbled with blood, —her eyes glazed, and her features convulsed into a wild paroxysm of insanity. When she saw herself discovered, she gibbered, made mouths, and pointed at them with her bloody fingers, with the frantic gestures of an exulting demoniac.

It is hardly suprising that this horror story should have been written, or rather dictated, when Scott was in an almost continual opium stupor, taking as much as two hundred drops of laudanum and six grains of opium a day to relieve the pain of a stomach ailment. Afterward, when he had recovered from both the treatment and the disease, he was unable to remember any details of what he had written, and found the results "monstrous gross and grotesque."

All the literary opium eaters—nota-

Tasso in the Madhouse *was painted by Eugène Delacroix in 1824 and, above, in 1827. Tasso, the sixteenth-century Italian poet imprisoned for insanity, became a kind of culture hero to Delacroix and his contemporaries.*

bly Coleridge, Crabbe, and De Quincey—wrote about lunacy and hallucination, but they were a long way from being the only ones who were attracted to the theme: some of the most eminently sober and even-keeled of writers introduced mad scenes in their work, often as much for stylistic as for psychological reasons. On the operatic stage, where there was a near epidemic of lunacy, it afforded composers a marvelous opportunity to write delirious music for the coloratura soprano.

More often, however, madness had a deeply rooted allegoric purpose in romantic art. The artist feels an instinctive brotherhood with the madman in his isolation, which so closely parallels his own increasing alienation from the "normal" nineteenth-century world. This is not to imply that the romantics were mad—some of them were—or that madness is the prevailing tendency in their work: there are a great many rationalist currents in romanticism that run counter to this one. But the romantic is at least aware that he is no longer living in an age of reason, and he recognizes some of his own features in the grimaces of the lunatic. Eventually he may conclude that the whole

of human life is madness, or that he has been born into a mad age. "I was born in 1813," says Sören Kierkegaard, "in that mad year when so many other mad bank-notes were put into circulation, and I can be best compared to one of them."

The comparison is not as unflattering to him as it would have been a century earlier, for the romantics had revived the ancient belief that madness is orphic knowledge. Insanity, says Charles Nodier, the teacher of Victor Hugo and Alfred de Musset, represents an upward step in the evolution of consciousness:

Lunatics . . . occupy the highest degree of the scale that separates our planet from its satellite, and since they communicate to this degree with a world of thought that is unknown to us, it is only natural that we do not understand them, and it is absurd to conclude that their ideas lack sense and lucidity, since they belong to an order of sensations and comprehensions which are totally inaccessible to us, with our education and habits.

Nodier also wrote that one meets the most reasonable people in the madhouse. This is a time-honored literary conceit, even older than *Don Quixote,* and one to which most of the visionary writers were inclined to subscribe. Blake felt that way about Bedlam, and noted that "there are probably men shut up as mad in Bedlam, who are not so: that possibly the madmen outside have shut up the sane people."

A reasonably good case could be made for the thesis that Blake himself was mad, in a harmless way. He saw visions, tipped his hat to the apostle Paul, spoke of having had conversations with Milton, and drew "visionary heads" of, among others, the "Man who instructed Mr. Blake in Painting &c in his Dreams."

At a time when the line between genius and insanity was being ever more finely drawn, madness was obviously more than just a theme for painters and poets: it became a recognized mode of romantic destiny. Friedrich Hölderlin, the greatest of the German visionary poets, spent nearly forty of his seventy-three years as an incurably withdrawn mental patient. Donizetti, the composer of mad scenes in half a dozen operas, lost his mind at forty-seven and was committed to an asylum near Paris. Gérard de Nerval, the French storyteller and poet, was institutionalized several times before he finally committed suicide. Robert Schumann, the German romantic composer par excellence, spent the last two years of his life in an asylum suffering from auditory hallucinations. Nikolaus Lenau, the leading Austrian poet of the epoch, died after six years in an asylum. And the Marquis de Sade, one of the great *provocateurs* in the underground movement against reason, spent many years of his life in prisons and asylums as punishment for private visions that proved to be far less cruel than those that became public policy under the Terror.

In his psychoanalytic study of *Madness and Civilization* the French historian Michel Foucault describes Sade's case as a key to the new mental images that emerged at the end of the eighteenth century, among them "the complicity of desire and murder, of cruelty and the longing to suffer, of sovereignty and slavery, of insult and humiliation." In Foucault's view, the dialectics of sadism correspond to the passions of the age:

Sadism is not a name finally given to a practice as old as Eros; it is a massive cultural fact which appeared precisely at the end of the eighteenth century, and which constitutes one of the greatest conversions of Western imagination: unreason transformed into delirium of the heart, madness of desire, the insane dialogue of love and death in the limitless presumption of appetite. . . .

Obviously, it isn't necessary "to be in a habitual state of licentious insanity" (as Sade's police record described him) before one can write about it; the authors of some of the maddest mad scenes were unequivocally sane. But there were more than a few who wrote

H. W. DONNER, *The Browning Box*

This macabre drawing shows the poet Thomas Beddoes as a skeleton clad in academic robes. It was drawn in 1847 by a ten-year-old child—the son of Beddoes's executor—two years before the poet succeeded in poisoning himself.

about insanity because they had a strong streak of it in themselves. Heinrich von Kleist, the great poet of the German romantic theatre, belongs to this category: he pictured the world as a stage battleground on which to act out his sexual fantasies. The climactic scene of Kleist's masterpiece, *Penthesilea,* is a kind of inverted prophecy of the sadistic finale with which he was to end his own life: in 1811, shortly after his thirty-fourth birthday, he shot his mistress and himself.

Penthesilea, queen of the Amazons, is a neo-Grecian version of that familiar romantic figure, *la belle dame sans merci*—a man-eating woman who destroys her lover in a sudden fit of feminist resentment. She has met Achilles on the battlefield and yielded him her heart, and for a time love triumphs over war. Then, while the nuptial feast is being made ready, her Amazon blood lust surges up again. Tracking Achilles with her hounds, she shoots him through the throat just as he is about to throw himself at her feet:

He falls . . .
yet still he lives, the most unfortunate of men,
despite the arrow jutting far out from his neck;
choking and groaning, he picks himself up,
  pitches forward,

and rises once again, and tries to flee.
But she cries kill!—kill, Tigris! kill, Leane!
kill, Dirke! Melampus! Sphinx! kill, Hyrkaon!
and falls on him—with the whole pack, O Diana!
and seizes him, seizes his helmet crest,
and pulls him to the ground, a bitch-hound
  among hounds,
one striking at his breast, the other at his back,
till the ground trembles with his fall.
He, wallowing in the purple of his blood,
touches her gentle cheek and cries:
"Penthesilea! my bride! what are you doing?
is this the feast of roses that you promised me?"
But she—the lioness has heard him,
the ravenous cat who prowls
the snowy wastelands, howling after game—
she pounces, tearing the armor from his body;
and now she sinks her teeth into his white
  breast,
she and the dogs, her rivals;
Oxus and Dirke drive their fangs into his right,
she into his left side; when I came upon them,
the blood was dripping from her mouth and
  hands.

This is a scene that left most of Kleist's contemporaries speechless with horror. His penchant for cruel and unusual punishments anticipates the Theatre of Cruelty, with which another mad genius of the stage, Antonin Artaud,* attempted to reform the theatre of the twentieth century. Certainly he would have agreed with Artaud that cruelty is what cements the world together, that cruelty "molds the features of the created world." Kleist represents an extreme case of the artist who identifies himself with madness and who compels his nightmares to represent him on the public stage.

Most of the other romantics who wrote about insanity preferred playing a kind of cat-and-mouse game with it. "I have pray'd/For madness as a blessing," Byron says, speaking through the mask of the melancholy *Manfred;* though one of the sanest men who ever lived, he was not averse to giving the impression that he was "Mad, bad and dangerous to know" (as Lady Caroline Lamb was delighted to attest).

Such literary posturings sometimes led to a denouement where real madness took over from the simulated kind. Only rarely, however, does anyone give us an insider's view of insanity—perhaps because it is so difficult to write

*See "A Vocation for Madness," which appeared in the Spring, 1970, issue of HORIZON.

coherently about incoherence. The one romantic writer who speaks eloquently and from personal experience about what it actually means to go mad is Gérard de Nerval, who manages to be both poetic and explicit about his psychotic interludes.

Nerval was thirty-three when he suffered his first severe attack of hallucinations in 1841. One evening as he was walking through Paris he felt himself magically attracted by an eastern star. As its magnetism drew him onward he began shedding his "terrestrial garments" and scattering them on the sidewalk. "The roadway seemed to lead continually upwards and the star to grow bigger," he writes in *Aurélia.* "Then I stood still, my arms outstretched, waiting for the moment when my soul should break free from my body, attracted magnetically by the rays of the star. A shudder went through me. Regret for the earth and for those I loved there gripped my heart, and so ardently within myself did I beseech the Spirit drawing me up towards it that it seemed as if I went down again among men. A night patrol surrounded me."

He spent the night in jail, still hallucinating. Friends came to fetch him in the morning, and he was transferred to a private clinic, where the visions continued for many weeks. The continents opened up before him; he saw to the ends of the earth, "beyond the Mountains of the Moon and ancient Ethiopia," to Granada and the banks of the Rhine, but "Everywhere the suffering image of the eternal Mother was dying, weeping, or languishing." It occurred to him, then, that he was embarked on the kind of spiritual journey which the ancients must have regarded as a descent into hell.

After eight months his visions had subsided and Nerval seemed cured. He recovered sufficiently to make a journey to the Near East, but there were to be further schizophrenic episodes, and he committed suicide in 1855. According to his doctor, Emile Blanche, "Gérard de Nerval hanged himself be-

cause he saw his madness face to face."

At least his insanity seems to have been no impediment to his poetry; on the contrary, it led him to that curious concept, *supernaturalisme,* which was to exert a powerful influence on the early surrealist poets. T. S. Eliot acknowledged another sort of debt when he quoted from him in *The Waste Land* —the desolate lines in which Nerval describes himself as *"El desdichado,"* a man abandoned by fate, *"Le prince d'Aquitaine à la tour abolie."* In the same poem Nerval speaks of the "black sun" of his melancholia, and yet, precisely like an exiled prince, he takes a certain defiant pride in his outcast state. Madness, he suggests, is a gift that is not to be taken lightly, since it leads to the liberation of the poet's second sight.

This is very close to Georg Büchner's view of insanity as an ecstatic dance of freedom that mimes man's revolt against the restraints of civilization. Büchner's madmen are heroes, not villains, and their actions anticipate R. D. Laing's contention that madness is often nothing more than a desperate bid for liberty. The title role of Büchner's play *Woyzeck* (better known in this country in Alban Berg's operatic version, *Wozzeck*) presents a case

Heinrich von Kleist, whose portrait this is, was the wild man of German romantic poetry. In 1808 he wrote a play about a murderous bride; three years later, at the age of thirty-four, he proceeded to kill both his mistress and himself.

in point, where madness is the only possible solution to an otherwise insoluble problem.

And Büchner's *Lenz*—perhaps the finest short story in the German language, certainly of the romantic century—is one great, never-ending mad scene. It is based on the life of the young poet Reinhold Lenz, a close friend of Goethe's, who lived in a mountain village under a clergyman's care while slowly going mad. No one, not even Nerval, has succeeded as well as Büchner in capturing the terrible tension and impatience of insanity:

But only as long as there was light in the valley were things bearable to Lenz; as evening came on he was overcome by a strange anxiety, he felt he wanted to run after the sun. As his surroundings grew darker in shadow, everything seemed dreamlike to him, repugnant; anxiety took hold of him like a child who must sleep in the dark; he felt as if he were blind. And now it grew, this mountain of madness shot up at his feet; the hopeless thought that everything was a dream spread itself out in front of him; he clung to all solid objects. Figures rapidly passed him by, he pressed toward them; they were shadows, life withdrew from him, his limbs were numb. He spoke, he sang, he recited passages from Shakespeare, he grasped at everything that might make his blood flow faster, he tried everything, but—he was cold, cold!

As a sustained exploration of madness in literature, Büchner's *Lenz* is eclipsed only by an American novel that deals with insanity on the sea rather than in the mountains and has the hero's blood running hot rather than cold when the lunacy is upon him:

Often, when forced from his hammock by exhausting and intolerably vivid dreams of the night, which, resuming his own intense thoughts through the day, carried them on amid a clashing of frenzies, and whirled them round and round in his blazing brain, till the very throbbing of his life-spot became insufferable anguish; and when, as was sometimes the case, these spiritual throes in him heaved his being up from its base, and a chasm seemed opening in him, from which forked flames and lightnings shot up, and accursed fiends beckoned him to leap down among them; when this hell in himself yawned beneath him, a wild cry would be heard through the ship; and with glaring eyes Ahab would burst from his state-room, as though escaping from a bed that was on fire.

As Herman Melville says earlier in *Moby Dick,* "Human madness is oftentimes a cunning and most feline thing. When you think it fled, it may have but become transfigured into still subtler form." When he himself pursues this essence to its roots in totem and taboo, it leads him, as it has the earlier romantics, to that dark and mysterious realm of the subconscious, "where far beneath the fantastic towers of man's upper earth, his root of grandeur, his whole awful essence sits in bearded state . . ." But Melville did not possess the temperament to pull the beard of the king he found there enthroned; that literary feat was reserved for the Englishman Thomas Lovell Beddoes, whose five-act black comedy *Death's Jest Book* is probably the most bizarre piece of writing produced during the romantic age.

Beddoes, who was born in 1803 and committed suicide in 1849, belongs to the great tradition of English eccentrics. He left Oxford to go to Germany and Switzerland, where he spent more than twenty years studying anatomy and dabbling in literature. If Keats was "half in love with easeful death," Beddoes was wholly in love with it, and *Death's Jest Book* is his obsessional masterpiece—a sprawling, blood-drenched fantasy into which he projected his most sadistic dreams about corpses and ghosts and madness and revenge. His style is archaic, modeled on the Elizabethan and Jacobean dramatists, and the action, centered on the revolt of the court fool, takes place at a German court in the Middle Ages. This sense of being twice removed from reality in time and language gives Beddoes's work a strangely psychotic quality, as though it were taking place in the hermetic asylum of his mind's eye:

FOOL: I will now speak a word in earnest, and hereafter jest with you no more: for I lay down my profession of folly. Why should I wear bells to ring the changes of your follies on? Doth the besonneted moon wear bells, she that is the parasite and zany of the stars, and your queen, ye apes of madness? As I live I grow ashamed of the duality of my legs, for they and the apparel, forked or furbelowed, upon them constitute humanity; the brain no longer; and I wish I were an honest fellow of four shins when I look into the note-book of your absurdities. I will abdicate.
THE LADY: Brave! but how dispose of your dominions, most magnanimous zany?
FOOL: My heirs at law are manifold. Yonder minister shall have my jacket; he needs many colours for his deeds. You shall inherit my mantle; for your sins, (be it whispered,) chatter with the teeth for cold; and charity, which should be their greatcoat, you have not in the heart. . . . But now for my crown. O cap and bells, ye eternal emblems, hieroglyphics of man's supreme right in nature; O ye, that only fall on the deserving, while oak, palm, laurel, and bay rankle on *their* foreheads, whose deserts are oft more payable at the other extremity: who shall be honoured with you? Come candidates, the cap and bells are empty.
THE LADY: Those you should send to England, for the bad poets and the critics who praise them.
FOOL: Albeit worthy, those merry men cannot this once obtain the prize. I will yield Death the crown of folly. He hath no hair, and in this weather might catch cold and die . . . Let him wear the cap, let him toll the bells; he shall be our new court-fool: and, when the world is old and dead, the thin wit shall find the angel's record of man's works and deeds, and write with a lipless grin on the innocent first page for a title, "Here begins Death's Jest-book."

An anatomist by training and pathologist by instinct, Beddoes subjected death and madness to the most minute clinical investigation before giving them, as it were, a clean bill of health. It is said that he was constitutionally unable to finish anything, but after several unsuccessful suicide attempts—the next-to-the-last cost him a leg—he was finally able to put an end to his life with curare. "I am food for *what I am*

good for*—worms," begins his suicide note, in which he thoughtfully bequeathed fifty bottles of Moët 1847 champagne to a cousin "to drink my health in." Even in this last ironic gesture there is a hint of that arcane sense of mummery that makes *Death's Jest Book* such a lovely piece of absurd theatre.

The madman as a symbol is a living reproach to the skeptical, scientific view of man and the universe, which underlies everything that used to be known as Progress, and which, even in the 1800's, was felt to be badly in need of reappraisal. The madman as metaphor is also the one who opens the trap door to that nether world where fiction and reality have quite a different relationship from the one we know from the daily newspapers. And it is here, far beneath the fantastic towers of man's upper earth, that the artist may hope to reclaim his lost legacy of dreams, myths, and mystic flights of imagination.

This is a search in which he has invested an almost Messianic longing. It has gone on uninterruptedly for two hundred years, in the work of Dostoevsky and Kafka and Joyce, Baudelaire and Robbe-Grillet and Nabokov. Still the madman remains with us as one of the great themes of art: indeed, all art is now mad, madder than ever, quite mad! if regarded from the standpoint of a "sane" observer, circa 1800. Yet the artist has no choice but to continue the search. He knows, of course, that dealing with madness is playing with Promethean fire. "It is not otherwise possible," says Goethe. "Whoever stands thus at the edge of the abyss has to die or go mad; there is no mercy."

The Madhouse by Goya, opposite, was described by the painter as a "corral of madmen and two who are fighting, nude, with their keeper beating them . . ." Were it not for his black uniform, the keeper would be indistinguishable from his charges. Goya was stricken with temporary madness in 1792, about two years before he did this painting.

ON THE FOLLOWING PAGES: PAINTERS OF THE MAD SCENE

"The Madhouse"

"The House of Death"

William Blake: "From the Centre of His Own Crystal"

William Blake with the painter John Varley

If William Blake is among the fauna in the darker reaches of the romantic forest, it is not as a verifiable psychotic but as a visionary. In T. S. Eliot's words, "Blake was naked and saw men naked, and from the centre of his own crystal." One of the most limpid of English poets, Blake was an equally explicit painter—except that his very simplicity becomes puzzling. His paintings lack many of the conventional techniques of realistic art, but Blake was not a primitive and was quite capable of painting realistically—except that he did not care to. Nature, the great deity of Wordsworth, was to Blake a delusive goddess. What he wanted to paint were his visions of God and the truth he found in his own imagination. He had no taste for worldly pursuits. *The House of Death*, above, is his idea of what this earthly life is all about. A disembodied figure of Death and another representing Despair preside over a scene "Of gastly Spasm, or racking torture, qualmes/Of heart-sick Agonie, all feavorous kinds . . ." So runs the passage in *Paradise Lost* probably used by Blake as his text for this painting. He often painted from texts, as preachers preach from them.

Born in 1757, Blake spent most of his life in London, earning what little he could as a poet, painter, and engraver. When he was sixty, a group of young painters adopted him and cared for him during his last years. One of them, John Linnell, made the pencil sketch on this page showing the aged Blake with another of these disciples, John Varley. During this period Blake produced a series of *Visionary Portraits* to show his friends the kinds of supernatural visitors he was receiving daily. Among them was the spectral flea whose likeness appears on the opposite page. The flea told Blake that all fleas were inhabited by the souls of bloodthirsty humans. Blake died in 1827, singing on his deathbed of the heaven he saw before him.

"The Ghost of a Flea"

"Bridge of Chiros"

"A Great Soul Lapped in Majestic and Unearthly Dreams"

Such was the painter John Martin, at least in the opinion of the novelist Sir Edward Bulwer-Lytton and of most of his contemporaries. "Mad Martin," as he was called (for no better reason than for being the brother of a pyromaniac) was one of the most lauded painters of the early nineteenth century. Like Blake, he was no realist, preferring instead the landscapes of imagination. *Sadak in Search of the Waters of Oblivion*, a work of 1812, re-creates some immense and rocky isle of Martin's own dreams. In the foreground is "Sadak," who sets out to find the waters of forgetfulness. According to the legend, a jinni directs Sadak to his fearful destination at the edge of an abyss —just the spot for a good romantic shudder—then reappears, hurls him into the tides, and takes his leave. The *Bridge of Chiros*, engraved some fourteen years later, is another overwhelming landscape. This one is reminiscent of industrial England—a railroad bridge or a mine shaft might have been in Martin's imagination.

Martin thought the chief aim of the painter should be to astonish the viewer, by the sheer size of his canvas, if nothing else. He was a student of world history and believed in "catastrophism," the theory that the earth had taken its present form through a series of cataclysms. To the delight of his public, he re-created a number of these events on canvas. Princess Charlotte of England and Louis Philippe of France were among his warmest admirers.

Though Martin's reputation was never dampened by the waters of oblivion in his lifetime, it has been unfortunately drowned by them since. The handsome portrait of the artist seen at right was drawn by his son.

Portrait of John Martin

"Sadak in Search of the Waters of Oblivion"

The Lunacy of Richard Dadd

"The Child's Problem"

According to Sacheverell Sitwell, Richard Dadd was "the only good painter who worked through a lifetime of mental disease." *The Fairy Feller's Master-Stroke*, of which a detail appears at left, is his masterpiece, or at least his surviving masterpiece, for Dadd lived in insane asylums nearly half a century and much of his work was lost or destroyed. The painting depicts a strange world amid the creeping vines: fallen hazel nuts and stems of grass give scale to the miniature landscape. It is populated by, among others, the king and queen of fairies (center, top), two buxom women with winged hats (left), an odd couple (center) costumed in the mode of the 1840's, and a cross-eyed gnome hunched distractedly before the "fairy feller," whose axe will never fall. It is all as inexplicable as the title.

Born in 1817, Richard Dadd early proved to have great artistic gifts, which his adoring father had the means to encourage. The family even moved to London to enroll the young man at the Royal Academy. He was just beginning to be well known and to receive important commissions when a hallucinatory psychosis overwhelmed him. In 1843, aged twenty-six, he stabbed his father to death. Pronounced a criminal lunatic, he was locked away for the rest of his life. Ordinarily a gentle man, Dadd attracted the sympathy of a physician who urged him to paint.

Among his surviving drawings is the one above, entitled *The Child's Problem*. In it, a crazed little boy is advancing upon his sleeping father, whose head is partially shrouded. In the background hangs an engraving, famous in its day, of a black slave begging for his freedom; there is also a classical nude and a picture of a ship in a gale. The drawing surely contains a clue, however mysterious, as to why Richard Dadd became a patricide.

'The Fairy Feller's Master-Stroke"

"Principal Hobgoblin Painter to the Devil"

So said the critics of Henry Fuseli, and undoubtedly he was pleased. "I was born in February or March," he wrote, "it was a cursed cold month, as you may guess from my diminutive stature and crabbed disposition." His self-portrait, below, is crabbedness incarnate—beaky nose, bony fingers, bushy brows. He was known, even to friends, as "the terrible Fuseli," for he lived in perpetual anger. The rumor went around that he consumed a plate of raw meat each night at bedtime in order to make his dreams the more fearsome. Fuseli, however, was no lunatic, and his eccentric behavior had an element of showmanship about it. He had many devotees, among them William Blake, who praised his friend in a sardonic bit of doggerel:

> The only Man that e'er I knew
> Who did not make me almost spew
> Was Fuseli: he was both Turk & Jew—
> And so, dear Christian Friends, how do you do?

Fuseli shared and in large part instigated the taste for the macabre that characterized his age. *The Nightmare*, right, was painted in 1781 and made him internationally famous. A hundred years hence, an engraving of this frightful scene was to be found in the office of Sigmund Freud, who greatly admired it. The term "nightmare" originally meant a dream of being suffocated or crushed, and Fuseli interprets this literally: a fiend is squatting on the chest of his curvaceous victim, while his horse peers wildly through the bed curtains. The physiologist Erasmus Darwin also liked the painting, so much so that he paid tribute to it in verse:

> So on his Nightmare, through the evening fog,
> Flits the squab Fiend o'er fen, and lake, and bog;
> Seeks some love-Wilder'd Maid with sleep oppress'd,
> Alights, and, grinning, sets upon her breast.

Self-portrait by Henry Fuseli

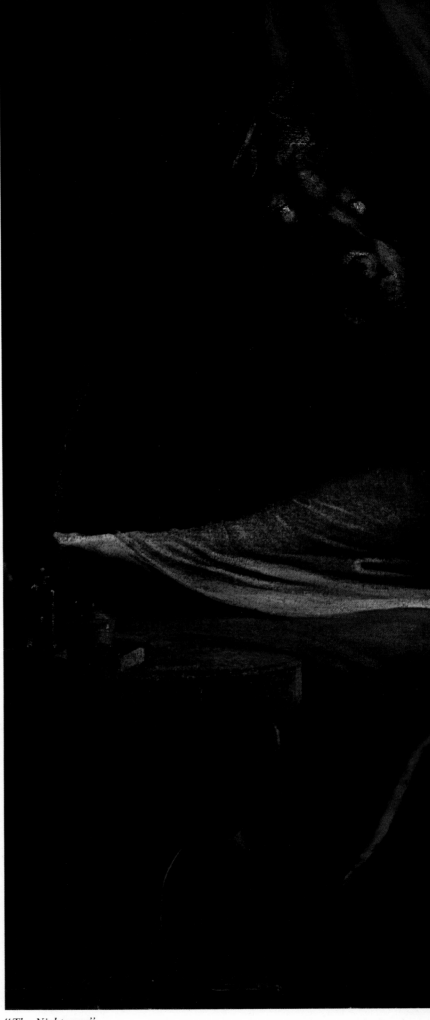

"The Nightmare"

THE ROAD TO UR

It wasn't fire or sword that
brought down
the most ancient of civilizations.
It was the silting
and salting of the fertile land
—man's first,
unheeded lesson in ecology

By FRANKLIN RUSSELL

*In a wasteland of marsh and sun-baked
mud a few miles from the Euphrates lie
the ruins and rubble of Ur, chief
city of ancient Sumer. Five thousand
years ago rich fields of wheat and
barley made this landscape green.*

SIR LEONARD WOOLLEY, *Ur Excavations*, VOL. 5; DRAWING OPPOSITE: SAME

HOUSE FOR A GOD

The Ziggurat of the Moon God, a stepped tower of brick surmounted by a temple, once dominated the collective life of Ur, which revolved around the worship of the god of the temple. At left is the ziggurat as it looked after Sir Leonard Woolley excavated it in the 1930's. Probably consisting at first of three platforms, the ziggurat was built by Ur-Nammu, a king of Ur who made himself ruler of all Sumer in 2125 B.C. The stele fragment opposite commemorates Ur-Nammu's act of piety: the top portion shows him pouring a libation for a seated god; in the lower portion he carries construction tools.

The sun spills across the Euphrates at dawn and hits the great ziggurat, a brick mountain rising from an ocean of dust. Approaching it from the east, I feel the sun's heat burning my back at the same instant that the ziggurat flames red in the sunlight. The moment is eerie, unearthly, and it confounds any attempt I might make to describe it.

This is the ziggurat of Ur-Nammu, one of the last of the Sumerian kings who ruled in southern Mesopotamia, now modern Iraq. Standing on top of the ziggurat, a kind of stepped tower, or pyramid, which was the distinctive Sumerian contribution to architecture, it is possible to look down on the ruins of Ur, a five-thousand-year-old city tumbled into a disorder of sun-dried bricks.

The place has always had a special fascination for me because here is compressed the essence of man as he refined the most sublime invention on earth, civilization itself. Here, where the sun at six thirty this morning is hot enough to scorch the skin on my forearms, the Sumerians transformed man's image of himself and started the whole machinery of urban civilization forward on its endlessly enigmatic journey.

Here, men first challenged nature with a boldness and success matched in human history only by the Americans some five millenniums later. Here was born the idea of creating a completely new geography in which man was indisputably the master of his environment, bending it to his will. Like our own, the Sumerians' need for material things was prodigious, and they made much more sophisticated use of techniques and tools invented several millenniums before.

Here, the wheel first rolled upon a gridwork of city streets and cuneiform writing was first inscribed on clay. The Sumerians were not merely master architects and superb hydraulic engineers, they were also the inventors of the military phalanx, the B-52 of its day, a devastating and seemingly omnipotent weapon. From out of their imaginations came deep-sea merchantmen, formalized schools, epic poetry, the arch, the city, traffic jams, pollution, and the world's first great crisis in ecology. It was here, not in Egypt, or Babylon, or Greece, or Rome, that men first codified rational laws to govern human behavior. They invented democracy, crude but recognizable, and the concept of empire, brutal and familiar.

Now, all around me there is a silence you find only in deserts and high mountains. The sun bakes the skin and the air shakes. The sky is clear and pale blue, dropping to a distant horizon that shows the mounds of other dead cities. At the foot of Ur-Nammu's monument, my Bedouin guide points to cuneiform marks on a crumpled brick wall. "Ibrahim," he says. "His house here."

Perhaps Abraham *did* live here thirty-seven hundred years ago, and perhaps Ur *was* a bustling port with ships moored not a hundred feet from where I stand. Perhaps this same sun *did* shine on the city's roofs and on the majestic march of irrigation canals. But this kind of imagining is easier in a library or a lecture hall, where the dreadful reality of the place does not intrude. The journey men made to reach this place cannot be rendered sensible merely by looking at it as an expression of a civilization's rise and fall. One must look to the earth itself, which supported man here, and then, groaning, let him drop.

To reach Ur by a road that has meaning for us today, it is necessary to leave the ruined city and move north and east along an uncertain path nearly fifty thousand years old. We are following the route of civilization back to its source. Instead of measuring monuments and chronicling the deeds of

A stele honoring the ziggurat's builder

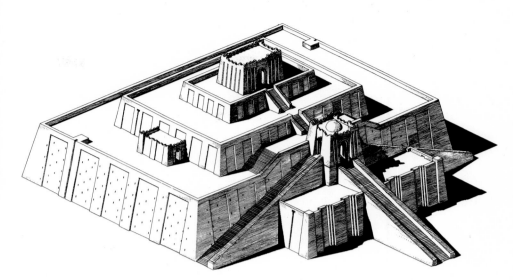

The ziggurat of Ur as it probably looked about 2000 B.C.

warriors, princes, gods, and kings, it makes more sense to look for those quiet events of natural history that took place unnoticed by most historians: how the grass grew, how the crops flourished, how the water flowed and the silt settled.

The facts are unreliable, the dates dubious, the order of events uncertain; but as I move eastward the landscape becomes more stimulating than the featureless plains of the Euphrates and the Tigris. I move along the banks of the Diyala, a tributary of the Tigris. For more than five thousand years life-giving water has been taken from this river for crops, first by the shadowy men of prehistory, then by Sumerians, Babylonians, Assyrians, Persians, Parthians, Mongols, Neo-Persians, Turks, and Arabs.

The river is a roadway leading to the Zagros Mountains, passing through scattered fields of rice, barley, and wheat, citrus orchards, and rows of date palms, then rising into treeless, rolling hills of grass. Flocks of sheep and cattle and goats graze on all sides. Nearchus, Alexander's lieutenant, traveled here more than twenty-two hundred years ago, and it impressed him as a place of "clear rivers and lakes, abundant rain and forests full of wild animals."

The forests and wild animals are harder to find today, but the grasses are the same and so are the abounding wild grains and fruits. This is a natural landscape for the nomadic hunter, the shepherd, the grain-and-fruit gatherer, the simple farmer. The hills roll on for miles as the altitude increases toward its eventual peak of more than fourteen thousand feet in the still-distant Zagros Mountains. Deep, narrow valleys run into the Diyala, and defiles and precipices increase as the air chills with height. In these valleys, I know, early hunters found protection from winter weather, and it is not hard to visualize their environment.

The ancient landscape is African in its sweep and scope, and its lions and leopards, cheetahs and hunting dogs, hyenas and jackals, make the resemblance more than superficial. But the true significance is that there are so many domesticable animals here—wild sheep, goats, pigs, asses—grazing among so many plants that yield edible grains—barley, wheat, oats. The steppes, foothills, uplands, and mountains are a kind of geographic tinderbox inviting the nomadic hunter to strike a spark.

From November to March the mountains gleam with snow and the steppe country provides good grazing. As the

heat and drought of summer grow unbearable on the plains and begin to steal into the hills, the animals and hunters move higher, toward the cooler mountain country where the grazing remains good. It does not need a lifetime of living here to understand the principles of rotational grazing, or to guess at the benefits to be gained from taming the wild animals.

But needed first are men who can change themselves, and a leisurely thirty thousand years or so pass while they take their first hesitant steps toward the plains. They barter natural asphalt mined in the tar pits of the northeastern steppes with men who live in the mountains of Turkey and use the asphalt to fit handles to their flint tools and weapons. In return, the traders get obsidian, from which they fashion their own tools and weapons. Trading increases the flow of ideas among men and helps power the movement toward a domesticated man.

Thirty-odd thousand years is long enough to change all previous agreements the men have made with their world. They tame the sheep, goats, and pigs. They develop and refine techniques of grazing. They breed selectively to improve their animals. They change the wild sheep's fur into wool

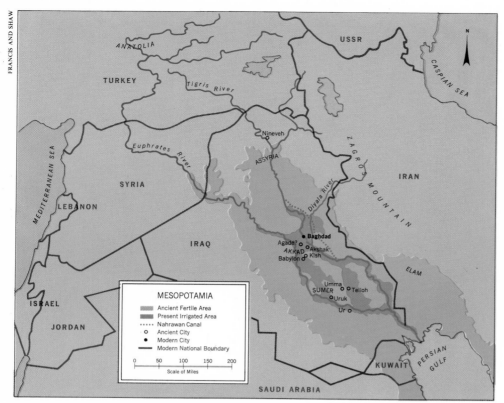

MESOPOTAMIA
- Ancient Fertile Area
- Present Irrigated Area
- ······ Nahrawan Canal
- ○ Ancient City
- ● Modern City
- —— Modern National Boundary

0   50   100   150   200
Scale of Miles

Sumerian civilization arose in southern Mesopotamia before 3000 B.C. As the Sumerian soil was exhausted, the centers of power shifted northward toward the areas that were still fertile.

and transform the pig from a lean, fast runner into a slow, fat waddler. They harvest wild fruits and grains, barter them for meat or tool materials, and watch for mutations in the wild plants that will give them more and bigger seeds.

When these barley seeds develop, domesticated to produce six rows of seed instead of the two that the wild grain produces, they eventually reach the hot plains flanking the Diyala and are watered by bucket. The dusty earth reveals itself as incredibly fertile. From a single seed, the harvester gets a two-hundredfold increase.

But hill farmers, shepherds, nomads, and traders are scarcely the kind to build awesome monuments to gods in hellish deserts. It is easy to water a garden plot, another thing to irrigate a farm. The amount of land that can be irrigated is limited both by muscle and by ambition. Men settle along the Diyala and the Tigris, and along the Euphrates, where the riverbanks are low. They suffer in the heat of the plains while the other men roam or work in the cooler uplands.

Sometime after 6000 B.C. the plains-

men consolidate themselves into larger, better organized communities, with some of their kind finding a haven at the southern end of the plains, in the hottest of all country, near and among the fever-ridden marshes of the Tigris-Euphrates delta. The fertility of the river-borne silt is phenomenal, and man intensifies his farming. He co-operates with scores, then hundreds, perhaps even thousands, of his fellows and begins to build irrigation systems with channels quite far from the water source and reservoirs to hold flood waters until they are released into the fields weeks later.

Little is known about these earliest farmers of the Tigris-Euphrates delta. At first they lack metal, and a system of writing, and most of the equipment necessary to build a great civilization. They find that their irrigation is no open-ended contract for success. The farther the water is moved from its source, the more difficult it becomes to maintain the dikes, ditches, and channels needed to carry it. There are proliferating problems of riparian rights, of land law and other social controls.

Added to these are the dangers of flooding, which can wreck everything, the attacks of marauding nomads, who can seize the harvest, and pestilence, which can make maintenance of the system impossible.

The irrigation people hold a golden key to the future of man, but it is hard to bring them truly to life, impossible to measure their success. They leave the broken shards of their distinctive pottery in the silty earth, along with the remains of thousands of sickles made of sun-baked clay. But their power grows continuously, and they have a sense of the monumental long before they can speak to us in writing. A thousand of them can work together for five years to build a massive temple, yet they seem to find no special need for a king unless there is a war emergency or some other danger, and they govern themselves through councils of free men.

By 3500 B.C. the southern plains are dominated by the Sumerians, a short, stocky, black-headed race of people whose origins are obscure ("We come from where the sun rises"). If they are not the product of the environment, they are immigrants who understand how to increase its exploitation to the maximum. They grow wheat and barley in equal proportions. They extend irrigation systems, survive crippling floods, and laboriously build civilization in a loosely connected comity of city-states.

The genius of Sumer is in its cities, but its powerhouse remains an ecological one, that extraordinary link to the mutated grain, to the dormant fertile soil, to the road begun in the foothill country of the Zagros Mountains. The farmer is the silent hero of the great civilization growing above him. He cultivates his fields with meticulous care, using mallets to break up its clods, leveling it as flat as a table, coaxing bumper crops with three, four, or five floodings of irrigation water.

As the centuries roll on, the farmer learns that fertility is diminished when land is cropped without fertilizer. He rests his fields and grazes them, but even this does not restore the fertility completely. He knows, however, that when the river floods, his irrigation canals carry silt as well as water, and the silt is spread across the depleted fields. "Behold," the farmer says, "the inundation has come and the land is restored."

As a former farmer myself, I can watch his work with admiration, and with some compassion. When he floods his flat fields, evaporation begins immediately, causing the calcium and magnesium in the water to precipitate as salts. The soil contains particles of clay, torn loose from mountain origins along with topsoil silt. These particles attract sodium ions, causing them to break down into even smaller particles. The farmer understands that when he overfloods, he sours his fields. But he does not understand the grand process, continuing over hundreds of years, in which the gradual erection of a near-to-impervious barrier prevents the soil from absorbing water, and so increases the rate of evaporation and the deposition of more salts. The road to Ur-Nammu's ziggurat, therefore, is a journey through the earth itself. The edifice of civilization, in these terms, is less subject to the king's will than it is to the health of the earthworm.

By this time, I have moved out of the foothills of the Zagros and am again heading south across the alluvial plains toward Ur. To reach this point of understanding, I have moved four hundred miles in distance and some forty-three thousand years in time from the hill country where the road to the ziggurat begins.

Now, I pause at the site of Telloh, one of the cities in the ancient Sumerian state of Lagash, about fifty miles north of Ur. Here, it is possible to take a closer look at the kind of urban miracle erected on this foundation of the soil. Here, again, is the same deadliness of landscape, seen now from the ruins of the great temple of Ningirsu, the god of Telloh. Although his temple is now nothing more than a fifty-foot mound of rubble, it is a symbolic point

from which to view the Sumerian state at its zenith. When the temple was built in the third millennium B.C., the people of Lagash had been farming their land for a thousand years. Their city of Telloh sprawls for more than two miles along the banks of a great waterway that is visible now as an empty declivity in the dust.

The idea of the state, founded on phenomenal soil fertility and abundant water supplies, is fought to a resolution in Lagash. It is a bastion against hill barbarians, an incubator of high culture, imperialism, and exploitation. It covers about eighteen hundred square miles and holds about two hundred and fifty thousand people. The soil is indeed fertile. Lagash has a population density equivalent to about five billion people in the United States.

Every changeless facet of civilized society is expressed here. The center city of Telloh covers about four square miles, and trudging through the dust and sand, I imagine its ancient appearance. Outside the walls there is a hodge-podge of tumble-down buildings, reed hovels, even burrows in the ground. "The poor are always with us," the Sumerians are fond of saying. Blind beggars importune on all sides as the city's walls loom up. Inside the gates, the city is chaotic, unplanned, cramped—a mixture of narrow streets and walkways hardly wide enough for a donkey. The houses are tiny and the press and noise of people is daunting.

It is the reality of the city that dominates the view of the Sumerian civiliza-

This copper figurine shows an early chariot drawn by four onagers.

tion. The eighteen hundred square miles of cropland do not figure in the history books. Instead, there appears a disciplined, structured society dominated by the god, the king, the priests, and the patricians. But it is an oddly appealing society. Slaves buy their freedom, fight court cases, marry. Children argue with teachers. Ombudsmen cut down on the clutter of trivial civil court cases.

These people admire wealth, possessions, good food, yet their proverbs scorn this crass appreciation of the good life. Possessions, they say, are sparrows in flight with no place to land. Money guarantees nothing. Gold and food may give happiness, but a man with neither is more likely to have peace of mind. They are contemptuous of men who build like lords but then are forced to live like slaves. Abstinence, even poverty, they insist, can create contentment. They enjoin you to keep your mouth shut when in doubt. Don't cross your bridges until you come to them. Don't fantasize. Remember that love builds and hate destroys. And don't forget that a sweet word is everybody's friend.

The contradictions between the adages glorifying the simple life and the realities of abundant living are richly evident here. Through the narrow window of a one-story streetside house a wealthy family can be seen drinking from silver goblets shaped by an artist with an exquisite sense of line. A palace musician plays his lyre, an ornate, multistringed instrument as big as a cello and inlaid with carnelian and lapis lazuli. Regal-looking women walk through shaded courtyards wearing headdresses made of meticulously delicate beaten-gold leaves, their jewelry tinkling on their necks and wrists and ankles.

This is the surface veneer dominating the history. But already, by this time, there are warnings of ecological trouble. As a result of about a thousand years of irrigation, of millions of tons of water seeping down into the subterranean water table, the salt content of the underground waters has increased steadily. Wells that had once sustained entire villages are now undrinkable. Occasionally, when irrigation is especially intensive, or when there are long rains and floods, the water table rises until it reaches the roots of the crops and kills them.

Yet the civilization flourishes. It thrives despite the fact that in the previous thousand years the wheat crop has gradually diminished to only about a sixth of its former abundance. Wheat is intolerant of saline soil, and barley, which is less intolerant, replaces it wherever possible. But by 2500 B.C. yields of many crops are declining. Drainage ditches become clogged with rotting vegetation and provide a shelter for breeding mosquitoes, which multiply in great numbers and spread malaria among the farmers, weakening them so that they are less able to maintain the ditches. The water tables rise ominously, salinity becomes stronger, and the supply of food dwindles even further. In the crowded cities, bacteria thrive on the mix of human debris.

The civilization can survive only if the land remains rich, or if its productivity can be increased, or if the territory under cultivation can be extended. A king of Lagash, Eannatum, finds himself caught between the twin priorities of trying to conserve his irrigation supplies, partially under the control of a northern city-state, Umma, and of fighting expansionist wars. He brings the city-state of Uruk, a near-western neighbor, under his rule. He marches south on Ur and conquers it. He moves east and subjugates the Elamites, a foothill people with pretensions to civilization.

But he needs more cultivated land, with his crop yields declining and his demands rising. He turns his mass of workers to the construction of a great canal. In the middle of this project, the Elamites come down from the hills and attack him. He drives them off and returns to canal work, but before long he must fight two northern city-states, Kish and Akshak, which combine to invade his country. He beats them off, too, only to be hit by the Elamites once more. He smashes them, but is then forced to turn and fight the northerners again. He wins this last battle, but he cannot now finish his canal before his death. His son Entemena completes it and links it up with the Tigris. Because his canal network now joins the Tigris and the Euphrates, he acquires the awesome ability to swell or diminish the flow of either river at will.

The productivity of the soil has provided wealth, but it is an ambiguous blessing to any people lucky enough to possess it. The people of Lagash find themselves forced to pay for both expensive wars and massive public-works programs. There are taxes on divorce, on trade, on production, on income, on death. The penalties for late payment of taxes become more savage, and this is only a step from the outright seizure of livestock, of produce, even of a man's personal belongings. At the same time, war, or its threat, provides an excuse for authoritarian controls, including the draft, travel restrictions, and the erosion of civil liberties.

This repression leads logically to

A stone statue of Gudea, governor of the state of Lagash, depicts him as a grave and prayerful man: the ideal Sumerian ruler.

corruption, to periods of reform, to corruption again, and thence to what seems a rational solution of the problem: a coalition, an empire of city-states. A king of Uruk, Lugalzaggisi, subjugates all of Sumer. He says he will bring peace. He will stop the endless boundary disputes, the feuds over irrigation rights. His chroniclers note that all Sumer rejoices under his rule.

But Lugalzaggisi is merely an inspiration to a man with a better idea. Sargon, a Semite, not only seizes united Sumer, but extends his empire from the Persian Gulf to the Mediterranean, and his ships reach India and Africa. He builds the most glittering city on earth, Agade, in the Akkad region, and 5,400 other human beings sit down to eat with him each day. Yet beneath his feet the salt builds up in the soil and there is a melancholy decline in crop yields.

In Entemena's time, about 2400 B.C., the fields were yielding 2,600 liters of barley per hectare. But the power of the soil is declining so rapidly that barbarian conquest, and the rise of Ur-Nammu and his creation of a one-hundred-year renaissance, are anticlimactic. Ur-Nammu builds his marvelous ziggurat, but now, in 2100 B.C., his fields are yielding only 1,460 liters of barley per hectare. By 1750 B.C. Sumer is finished. Babylon, exploiting northern land, becomes pre-eminent.

It would be heartening to record that the Babylonians learn something from Sumer, but they do not. Their power becomes prodigious. Herodotus is astonished by the hundredfold yields of their vast farmlands and by the immensity of their public works, but the salt moves in just the same, and the decline of the farmlands is a mammoth disaster from 1300 to 900 B.C. The locus of the civilization moves even farther north, to Assyria. Amazingly, the term of the good earth's fertility is not over. From about 150 B.C. the Parthians are at work along the Diyala again, and they create a prosperous civilization that continues under the Persians until A.D. 600.

In this period, the mighty Nahrawan Canal is built, an artificial river nearly two hundred miles long, dug in a great semicircle to flank the course of the Tigris, to cross the desert, to bridge other rivers, until it finally rejoins the Tigris one hundred miles south of Baghdad. This fantastic engineering project contributes to the success of the Persian empire, but its life is even shorter than that of the salted southern lands. In five hundred years of cultivation of the Diyala region, the deposit of irrigation silt raises the level of farmlands more than three feet, and the irrigation engineers find it harder and harder to get the grade necessary to keep the water flowing.

By 1100 the water can only reach fields through branch canals flanking the main canal, and gradually towns and cities shrink and disappear. By the time the Abbasside caliphate is nearing its end, the silting of the system is a disaster. When a new Mongol invasion under Hulagu Khan, grandson of Genghis, captures Baghdad in 1258 and kills the last Abbasside caliph, much of the great farmland of the Diyala is again desert.

And this is the way the land is left —silted, salted, desolate. In the south, the average Iraqi gardener, working his vegetable plot on the banks of the Euphrates, raises a meager yield, not one-twentieth of that of his Sumerian predecessors. The modern farmer tilling a field near the ruins of Babylon brings forth a crop that would make Herodotus laugh. The Diyala might yield again, but while ancient Persians could build a two-hundred-mile-long canal, a similar effort would bankrupt Iraq, a country depleted by more than five thousand years of exploitation.

But land *can* be desalinated, and the Food and Agriculture Organization of the United Nations has brought back into production some ancient, salinated farmland in parts of Pakistan's Indus valley, home of another long-dead civilization. FAO experts, working for some years in the Meso-

The troops of Lagash are shown above in a limestone stele trampling on the soldiers of the neighboring city of Umma. Except for brief periods of unification, such warfare between Mesopotamian city-states was endemic.

potamian plain, have found about 90 per cent of the arable land to be affected by salt or waterlogging. They have discovered the modern Iraqi farmers to be so far removed from the irrigation techniques of the past that they will have to be trained to work any reclaimed land. And reclamation is a tedious, expensive, and lengthy business of developing pilot areas, of leveling great sections of the plain, of perfecting drainage systems, and of continuing research. The work is under way, but the Iraqi farmer remains a miserable heir to the defeated land.

It is now late afternoon in the desert, and the mounds of old ruins cast squat, ugly shadows. There is just time for me to reach Ur before evening. Ur-Nammu's ziggurat looks even more unlikely, set in its empty landscape with a reddening sky behind it. At the top of the ziggurat again, I watch the sun dropping into the clean red line of the Arabian desert. A jackal appears out of a pool of shadow below.

Lugalzaggisi uttered a prayer when he saw his great empire knit together and working, and the words come to me now: "May the lands lie peacefully in the meadows; may all mankind thrive like plants and herbs; may the sheepfolds . . . increase; the good fortune which has been decreed for me, may it never alter; unto eternity may I be the foremost shepherd . . ."

The dream of eternity is itself eternal and does not change from generation to generation. It is seen most clearly among those who strive hardest for power, for perfection, for improvement. Ur-Nammu earns eternal fame with his mighty monument, but the landscape is reproachful. I leave the ziggurat; the sun disappears. Fine phantoms of dust scamper through the broken bricks of Ur.

As a student of man—and other species— in relation to nature, Franklin Russell has written for HORIZON *about birds on an island off Newfoundland (Summer, 1965) and about the pioneer ecologist George Perkins Marsh (Summer, 1968).*

ILLUSTRATIONS CONTINUED OVERLEAF

THE BURDEN OF THE GODS

The Sumerians stood in awe of their gods, whom they conceived as dwelling in the forces of nature—which might capriciously destroy men—as well as in man-made temples and figurines—where they might be cajoled into acting as humanity's protectors. The group of statues at left, found together in the ruins of a temple, are believed to represent a god and goddess (the tallest pair) in confrontation with human worshipers. The god of each city was looked upon as its owner, so that the Sumerian was a tenant as well as a servant of the divinity—"burdened with the toil of the gods that they may freely breathe." In return for human labor, the god was supposed to ward off malign events. Like the poorest fisherman, the city's king was regarded as a servant of the gods. The figurine pictured above shows the great ruler Ur-Nammu as a humble basket carrier.

A PRECARIOUS PROSPERITY

An offering of wheat

The Sumerians clearly understood that their civilization rested on the fruits of the earth. In the inlay panel from Ur above (the blue stone is lapis lazuli) the pleasures of peaceful life—feasting, drinking, listening to music—are sustained by a procession of abundance: men bearing fish from the river, carrying bales of grain, tending woolly sheep, driving asses and oxen. Yet the Sumerians knew, too, that abundance was a gift the gods could snatch away. And in a sense that is what they did. By 2000 B.C. barley yields had become meager in Sumer, and wheat, once used on Sumerian seals as an indication of prosperity, as on the seal shown on the opposite page, had almost ceased to grow in the saline, worn-out soil.

A farmer astride his ox

Golden helmet in the form of a wig

THE GOLD OF UR

In 1922 Woolley discovered at Ur one of the Sumerians' most spectacular treasure-troves. There, under a rubble heap, lay sixteen royal tombs, built at the base of deep pits. In each pit were neat rows of bodies; one held the remains of sixty-eight women—court musicians with their instruments, among which was the bull's-head harp shown opposite. Probably the women accompanied their ruler to the tomb and then took their own lives with poison. The objects on this page—the golden helmet, the onager, the goat peering from a gilded tree—all come from Ur, that great repository of early Sumerian wealth and artistry. By Ur-Nammu's day, the wasteful practice of human sacrifice had been abandoned.

An onager atop a harness ring

A goat in a gilded tree

The Flood

Where did all the water go? Was the ark big enough? For centuries learned
men debated these questions—until Agassiz and Darwin pulled the plug

The central panels of Michelangelo's ceiling of the Sistine Chapel begin—as you will no doubt remember—with God separating the Light from the Darkness; they end—as you may perhaps have forgotten—with a drunken old man being put to bed. Yet it is quite certain that Michelangelo intended no anticlimax. For the old man is Noah, survivor of the Flood and second father of mankind.

We are all, as the legend has it, sons of Noah, as we are of Adam, and the ark is our lifeline, "a Ship," as Thomas Burnet wrote in his *Sacred Theory of the Earth* in 1684, "whose Cargo was no less than a whole World; that carried the fortune and hopes of all posterity, and if this had perish'd, the Earth, for any thing we know, had been nothing but a Desert, a great ruine, a dead heap of Rubbish, from the Deluge to the Conflagration. But Death and Hell, the Grave, and Destruction have their bounds."

Death and hell, the grave, and destruction have their bounds: this, for more than two millenniums, was the central theological meaning of the Flood, for even the end of the world will not annihilate all things, but will herald the Judgment. Mankind was

As the great Flood recedes, exposing the bodies of the drowned, animals from the ark head for shore in a miniature from the Bedford Book of Hours done in 1423. On dry land again, Noah is shown with his family tending grapevines and getting drunk on the vintage.

saved physically in the person of Noah, as Christians believe it was later saved metaphysically in the person of Christ; "and the waters shall no more become a flood to destroy all flesh."

The story of Noah is a rich one, fertile in symbolic motifs. The Fall gave symbolic significance to the tree and the serpent, to fig leaves and feminine wiles; the Flood, by contrast, gives us symbols of peace and reconciliation, the ark and the dove, the olive branch and the rainbow. Noah became not only the first drunken old sailor but also the first farmer, for the other half of the Noah story seems to contain a reference to the Neolithic revolution, the transition from an economy of flocks and herds and hunting to the cultivation of the soil. Noah's sons, Shem, Ham, and Japheth, were taken as the ancestors, respectively, of the populations of Asia, Africa, and Europe.

The story is therefore a composite one, but it is the ark and the Flood that every child remembers. And rightly so, for it is a story that has held a profound significance for mankind for longer, probably, than any other in the world's history. It expressed the anxieties of the most ancient literate people of whom we have any record, the Sumerians of the third millennium B.C., and it was still a matter of deep anxiety, though in a more indirect fashion, for erudite geologists in the reign of Queen Victoria. Compared with Noah and his wife, Adam himself

is relatively modern, Oedipus a parvenu, and King Arthur practically the boy next door.

Just how ancient the story is was first appreciated a century ago, when, at a meeting of Biblical archaeologists in December, 1872, a young assistant at the British Museum named George Smith announced that among the Assyrian tablets being deciphered at the museum he had discovered an account of the Flood. He was referring to the epic of Gilgamesh, which is at least fifteen hundred years older than Homer, and which contains the story of Utnapishtim and his wife, who became the sole survivors of a universal deluge by building a boat. Stories of this kind are not uncommon in mythology, but in Gilgamesh the similarity to Noah is so striking that it can hardly be accidental. It seems likely, too, that it refers to some actual flooding of the valley of the Euphrates.

The archaeology of the region discloses signs of several inundations, any of which could have been the ultimate origin of Noah's flood. The British archaeologist Sir Leonard Woolley, digging at Ur in 1929, made a notable discovery. Beneath the layers of successive civilizations, Woolley found between eight and eleven feet of mud, without any trace of human occupation, and then, beneath that, the ruins of human dwellings. He was convinced that he had discovered the historical reality behind the legend of the Flood. If so, it was almost certainly the original also of the ancient Greek story of a universal deluge, from which Deucalion, son of Prometheus, and his wife, Pyrrha, alone escaped by boat to repopulate the world. In Greek mythology Deucalion's flood separates the primeval golden age from the succeeding age of mortal men. The Biblical flood, too, though less emphatically, seems to mark a similar boundary. Before the Flood, giants walked the earth and men lived almost a thousand years; subsequently, things contract to more homely dimensions. Paradise itself was engulfed, and the site of it lost to memory, as Milton's archangel prophesied to Adam:

Out of his place, pushed by the horned flood,
With all his verdure spoiled, and trees adrift,
Down the great river to the opening Gulf . . .
The haunt of seals, and orcs, and sea-mews' clang.

Instead there is a guarantee of a natural world, neither paradisiacal nor chaotic, but ordered, regular, and endurable, a setting for the human condition, the daily round, the annual cycle: "While the earth remaineth, seed-time and harvest, and cold and heat, and summer and winter, and day and night shall not cease." Adam, eating the apple, knew good and evil and condemned all his posterity to death and sorrow; Noah, cultivating the vine, merely discovered that strong drink makes you drunk.

Milton presented Noah as the archetype of God's elect, a stern Puritan elder, vainly calling a corrupt people to repentance. But there were other, less austere interpretations. Noah, carpenter and farmer, and the ark, a floating zoo with the naive ungainliness of a man's first boat, have long had for mankind a homely, domestic quality.

A cuneiform clay tablet inscribed around 650 B.C. gives a Babylonian version of the Flood.

One would, after all, scarcely be so reassured to find one's children playing Adam and Eve, or Abraham and Isaac. The story of the Flood recapitulates, in many respects, that of the Creation itself, but in a lower key and on a more human scale. It is the most reassuring of disaster legends.

In the Middle Ages this homeliness became the keynote of the Noah story, in folklore and in the numerous cycles of Biblical mystery plays performed in the medieval towns. Of the numerous traditions that came to cluster around the Biblical story, some were of Judaic origin, like the Oedipal one that makes Ham's uncovering of his father's nakedness a literal castration—what one nineteenth-century geologist primly referred to as "domestic disturbances in Noah's family, briefly mentioned in Holy Writ."

The medieval treatment of these "disturbances," however, became broadly comic. It was not only Chaucer's carpenter, tricked by his wife's lover into building an ark in expectation of a second Flood while the lovers enjoyed themselves in his bed, who was a comic figure; the Noah plays themselves were often treated as comedy. Noah's wife is made a voluble shrew, and he himself

is mocked by his family and neighbors for his unaccountable obsession with inland shipbuilding—a tradition that also appears in the Koran. Another common theme was the reluctance of Noah's wife to enter the strange boat:

In faith, I can not fynd
Which is before, which is behynd.

In medieval folklore she appears as a kind of second Eve, with a special intimacy with Satan. In one story Satan tries to sabotage the ark, getting a mouse to gnaw a hole in it: in another, he induces Noah's wife, before the Flood, to find out why Noah is building such a ship. Noah—characteristically—gets drunk and tells her, whereupon Satan burns the ark and Noah has to begin again.

The Reformation encouraged a new literalness and intensity in the study of the Bible, and through the Puritan emphasis on original sin and the corruptness of everything merely natural, it stressed anew the sense that men lived in a world in decline, blighted and far from the original design of divine perfection. "Even the Earth," wrote Luther, "which is innocent in itself, and committed no sin, is nevertheless compelled to bear sin's curse." The Flood had destroyed Eden and deeply scarred the face of the earth: "since the Flood mountains exist where fields and fruitful plains before flourished . . . For the whole face of Nature was changed by that mighty convulsion."

We find Bishop Burnet in the later seventeenth century writing that "this misshapen Earth we now inhabit, is the Form it was found in when the Waters had retir'd, and the dry Land appeared." The present earth, according to him, is "the image or picture of a great Ruine," "a World lying in its

rubbish." This was a lamentable falling off from the original arrangements: "the face of the Earth before the Deluge was smooth, regular and uniform, without Mountains and without a Sea." There was "not a wrinkle, scar or fracture in all its body"; its uniform soil was "a light earth mix't with unctuous juices."

Paradise, it is clear, was not merely a garden, but a seventeenth-century formal garden—a kind of global Versailles "divided into Regions or Walks"; a torrid zone "made a kind of gravel-walk in the middle, so there was a green Walk on either hand of it, made by the temperate Zones; and beyond these lay a Canal, which water'd the Garden from either side."

This view of the antediluvian earth and of the catastrophic effects of the Flood came to have a considerable theological importance. The Flood played the same part in relation to the admitted imperfections in the natural world that Adam's disobedience played in relation to the sorrows of the human condition: neither was directly chargeable to the original plan of the Creation, and the ways of God toward men were justified.

This justification became more, not less, important as Christians in the eighteenth and early nineteenth centuries tended to ground their faith

Sinners vainly flee the Flood in a detail from Michelangelo's Sistine Chapel panel.

more and more upon the evidences of design and divine benevolence exhibited in the physical world. The concept of the universal Flood, and its justification by "the great wickedness of the antediluvians," meant that one could pursue such arguments without fear that they would be turned against one. In the optimistic eighteenth century, nature came more and more to be regarded as essentially benign, a worthy product of the almighty Clockmaker's workshop, yet no qualms needed to be felt at the discovery of imperfections; either they were not really so or their ultimate cause was men's sin, and their immediate one, insofar as they related to the physical condition of the earth, was the Flood.

Burnet's book remained highly influential for more than a century, and one finds echoes of it in Victorian times. In the formation of the globe, one critic wrote, "there is scarce a trace of that beautiful, tasteful and economical design which we have a right to expect from the admitted qualities of the great Author, and his avowed object in the structure and report of it when newly finished." Mountains, in particular, being both untidy and uneconomical, must be the result of the catastrophe of the Flood.

But theological arguments based on the Flood had also to be geologic argu-

ments. One of the chief problems for geology, as it developed in the eighteenth and early nineteenth centuries, became the occurrence, extent, and consequences of Noah's Flood. Because of the divine assurance that it would never recur, the Flood has not entwined itself with men's deepest hopes and fears, as have, for example, the prophecies of the Book of Revelation. Yet, by the early nineteenth century it did come to hold a key place in educated men's explanations of the nature of their world, to such an extent that the credibility of religion itself seemed to have become involved. As one writer put it, "the whole system of revealed religion is ultimately connected with the veracity of Moses." The Flood became the central geologic fact of theology.

There were reasons besides theological necessity for the importance of the Flood in geology. When men first began to consider possible physical explanations of the earth's crust systematically, there were many facts that pointed to a universal flood, or perhaps, as people in prescientific ages tended to believe, a primeval sea covering the earth. Much geologic activity, as we now know, has been caused by water, though not by a great deluge; hills and valleys, gravel deposits, ravines and water gaps torn through the mountains, all testify to the past action of water upon the earth.

But what of the fossil remains of sea creatures that were found on mountains far from any coast? Ancient Greek geographers had recognized the organic and marine origin of such fossils, as had the medieval scientist Albertus Magnus. Leonardo da Vinci's universal curiosity had, predictably,

been aroused by them. Why, he asked, "do we find the bones of great fishes and oysters and corals and various other shells and sea-snails on the high summits of mountains?"

But such men were rare. Until the late seventeenth century the organic origin of fossils was not generally appreciated. They were thought of simply as "figured stones." How had they got their strange shapes? One theory held that God had created these replicas of his animal creations just as a demonstration of his creative powers. Another held that stones were sexual creatures and reproduced like plants, or even copulated and gave birth in pain and labor. Even as late as the mid-eighteenth century, Voltaire, in order to discredit inland marine fossils that seemed proof of the Biblical Flood, held that they were fishbones dropped by travelers, or by pilgrims and Crusaders on their way to the Holy Land.

But gradually the organic theory triumphed. Its high point as testimony for the Flood came, perhaps, in the early eighteenth century, when a Swiss professor, Johann Scheuzinger, announced the discovery of a genuine antediluvian human skeleton. Scheuzinger christened his skeleton *"Homo diluvii testis"*—man witness of the Flood—and referred to him as a "rare relic of the accursed race of the primitive world," adding piously, "Melancholy skeleton of an old sinner, convert the hearts of modern reprobates!" Unfortunately, the skeleton so addressed subsequently proved to be that of a giant salamander.

Nevertheless, the general recognition of the organic nature of fossils was an immense step forward, and it helped perhaps more than anything else to establish the Flood as a scientific hypothesis. True, there were qualifications that had to be made as time went by. Geology was undermining literal interpretations of the Biblical account of the Creation and extending the age of the earth far beyond the original estimate of six thousand years. Stratigraphy revealed that there must have

Building the ark: a medieval view

been not one but a number of successive inundations, or deluges, and men had to be content with regarding Noah's flood as simply the last of them. Nevertheless, by the early nineteenth century the actuality of the Flood, and its geologic importance, seemed virtually unchallengeable.

The notion of a universal flood had the authoritative backing of men like General Charles Gordon, the doomed hero of Khartoum, who spent part of his leave in the Holy Land searching for the landing place of the ark. Another of these darkly brooding Victorian men of action was Robert Fitzroy, an officer in the Royal Navy and governor of New Zealand, who is best known to us as the captain of Charles Darwin's ship the *Beagle*. There can have been few odder conjunctions than that of the young Darwin with Fitzroy, for on the voyage that led Darwin to the theory that was to shatter the literal, Biblical account of the Creation for good, Captain Fitzroy was feverishly debating with himself, and occasionally with Darwin, such matters as the exact dimensions of the ark, and attributing the extinction of the huge prehistoric mammals to their having been left out of it.

Among men of science, though the Flood was generally accepted, there remained awkward problems: Why were fossil shellfish found in their original beds? Where did all the water go? Was the ark big enough? The significance of

the first question had been recognized by Leonardo da Vinci, and after him by the seventeenth-century naturalist John Ray. As Leonardo pointed out, "If the Deluge had carried sea shells three or four hundred miles from the sea, they would be thoroughly mixed in heaps with many other things. But instead we find the oysters all together, and also see the snails, the squid, and the other shellfish lying together in death as they lay in hordes while living." Leonardo and Ray were therefore among the first to be right about both questions relating to marine fossils: they were organic in origin, and they were not relics of the Flood.

By the later seventeenth century it had been realized that if the Flood was to be used as a scientific hypothesis, it had better be itself credible as a physical occurrence. Yet the Flood appeared to be a physical impossibility. Clearly, forty days' rain alone could not have caused so vast a catastrophe. One of the most popular theories was that adopted by the astronomer Edmund Halley, who said it was connected with the passage of a comet. (Comets were much in the public mind since the celebrated one of 1680, named after Halley himself.) The most ingenious and influential explanation, however, was given by Burnet in his *Sacred Theory of the Earth*.

Burnet brooded on the hydraulics of the Flood like a plumber with a problem. What if the earth had been flatter "and so might the more easily be overflow'd, and the Deluge perform'd with less water?" Staring into the face of Chaos, Burnet arrived at an answer. Chaos, being a fluid mass, when it solidified would necessarily fall into a spherical shape, with the moisture enclosed within it, like the yolk of an egg— "the Mundane Egg" as Burnet called it. The smoothness of Paradise was thus strictly in accordance with the principles known to seventeenth-century mechanics.

But Paradise was doomed from its inception. For the earth, exposed to the eternal summer of the paradisiacal climate, would become dryer; cracks would appear, and the waters within, growing warmer, would begin to vaporize and need more room. The serpent, one feels, need not have bothered; the Garden of Eden was cracking at the seams in any case. "So we see all Vapours and Exhalations enclos'd within the Earth, and agitated there, strive to break out, and often shake the ground with their attempts to get loose." (San Francisco resembles Paradise in more ways than one.) Then the catastrophe: parts of the earth plunged into the abyss below, and the water inside, driven out with immense force, rose high above the land. When the great maelstrom of water subsided, some of it would remain on the surface as open sea, since the former cavity was now blocked in places by the fallen land. Nothing could be more satisfactorily Scriptural, Noachian, and scientific.

But could the ark have contained all the species of living things? And given that the fauna of various parts of the world, especially the Americas, differed widely from those of the central land mass, how were they gathered together for the occasion, and then dispersed again? As the Victorian geologist Hugh Miller wrote in his *Testimony of the Rocks* (1857): "The sloths and armadilloes,—little fitted by nature for long journeys—would have required to be ferried across the Atlantic to the regions in which the remains of the megatherium and the glyptodon lie entombed." Miller's solution was that the deluge was only partial, destroying corrupt mankind but not the entire world's animal population.

Burnet, almost two hundred years earlier, did not have the problem of fossil ancestors to contend with, but he had his own unorthodox answer: there may have been a second ark, an all-American one, full of sloths and armadillos. Earlier in the seventeenth century Sir Walter Raleigh, passing the weary hours of his imprisonment in the Tower of London by writing his *History of the World,* had produced an even more radical solution: the animals

Evidence of a Mesopotamian deluge, indicated by a stratum of silt between layers of debris, was discovered at Kish in 1929.

of the New World had evolved, since the Flood, from those of the Old.

But as men's knowledge of the animal species grew, the difficulties continued to increase. Miller admitted that even on the most generous estimate of the "Noachian cubit," the ark would only have been about one-seventh the size of the great Crystal Palace of 1851. Raleigh, like the painstaking old sea captain that he was, had carefully estimated the provisions required for the voyage, and the amount of stowage needed, but he had assumed the existence of a mere eighty-nine species. Nineteenth-century zoology knew better. As Miller pointed out, there were, for example, not one but two species of elephant, *Elephas africana* and *Elephas indicus,* thus immediately doubling the elephant population of the ark—clearly a serious matter. There were six, or possibly seven, distinct species of rhinoceros, twenty-seven of sheep, and fifty-one of deer. From having been merely the guardian of a pair each of the larger animals, Noah was beginning to look more like a floating cattle baron in an impressive way of business.

But Miller, in the 1850's, with his hypothesis of a partial deluge sufficient to destroy humanity, which salvaged the theological but not the geologic significance of the Flood, was fighting a rearguard action. For, from the 1830's onward, an alternative explanation of the earth's crust had been gaining ground,

which, relying on the results of ordinary deposition and erosion through countless millenniums, made the hypothesis of a universal and sudden catastrophe such as the Flood unnecessary. The final blow to the Flood as a geologic explanation was the realization in the 1840's, by the Swiss-American geologist Louis Agassiz, of the importance of the action not of great floods but of the ice sheets that had once covered the Northern Hemisphere—the slow advance and retreat of the great glaciers.

For a time, consternation was acute; seldom have men grounded their peace of mind so firmly on belief in a catastrophe. Until it was subsumed in the still larger Darwinian controversy, geology became one of the chief agents of the Victorian crisis of faith.

The agony has abated, of course, and few people now feel their spiritual lives imperiled by the rather local nature of an ancient Mesapotamian disaster. But it is the characteristic of a great myth to absorb the preoccupations of many ages. Recently, the distinguished anthropologist Edmund Leach has given an anthropological interpretation of the Noah story. What interests him is not primarily the Flood, but the Oedipal episode of the sin of Ham, according to Leach a literal act of homosexual incest, for which, by tradition, Ham was turned black and his posterity enslaved. The significance of Noah, it seems, thus lies not primarily in God's wrath and his covenant with man; not in antifeminist jokes about Noah's wife, nor as a paradigm of God's treatment of his elect. It is not an explanation of such geologic untidiness as mountains and potholes, nor the explanation of such paleontologic puzzles as marine fossils on high ground far from the sea. It is, rather, about those terrible twins of our own time, Sex and Race.

We should have guessed.

J. W. Burrow also contributed four essays to the Horizon Book of Makers of Modern Thought, *published this summer.*

The Young Lenin

By Leon Trotsky

A Doomed Author, A Wayward Manuscript

In 1933 Leon Trotsky was commissioned by the Doubleday publishing company to write a full-scale biography of Lenin, a task for which he was uniquely qualified. Trotsky had been Lenin's close ally and lieutenant in the Russian Revolution and, next to him, for some years the most important figure in the Bolshevik regime. The subsequent fates of the two revolutionary allies, however, could not have been more disparate. Lenin died in 1924. He became—and remains—the supreme, virtually deified hero of the Soviet Union. Trotsky, defeated by Stalin in a power struggle, vilified as a traitor, exiled in 1929, was literally written out of official Soviet history.

At the time of Trotsky's assassination in Mexico in 1940 by a Stalinist agent, his unfinished biography of Lenin had already disappeared and was presumed lost. In 1968, however, it resurfaced when the noted author Max Eastman (1883–1969) submitted his English translation of it to Doubleday & Company. The following account of young Lenin has been excerpted from Trotsky's long-lost and long-forgotten manuscript, to be published in July under the title *The Young Lenin*.

At the point where the narrative begins, Lenin's father, Ilya Nikolayevich Ulyanov, overcoming the savage handicap of humble birth, had become the superintendent of public schools in a district governed by the Volga River town of Simbirsk, "the most backward and provincial of all the Volga capitals," according to Trotsky. "Not a town but a graveyard," said the noted Russian author Goncharov, one of Simbirsk's two most illustrious natives. The other was Vladimir Ilich Ulyanov, the future Lenin, who was born there in 1870.

Members of the inner circle and outsiders, even those who were to become enemies, speak in nearly the same terms of the friendly and industrious character of the Ulyanov family, of the purity and honesty of their domestic relations, of the cheerful mood in the family dining room. The absence of humiliating want or of flabby excess, the continual vivid examples of duty and industry in the father, the active and tender vigilance of the mother, a common interest in literature and music—all these conditions were very favorable to the bringing up of healthy and firm-hearted children. . . .

In his personal make-up, his ways and manners, Ilya Nikolayevich was a far cry from the stereotype of the cut-and-dried bureaucrat. He was a very warm human being—sociable, alert, with a good sense of humor. During his endless journeys, when stopping at the estate of some liberal *zemstvo* member, he loved to open his heart in conversations about the life of the *gubernia* and especially its educational affairs. . . .

In 1874 Ilya Nikolayevich was appointed superintendent of public schools. By now several inspectors were his subordinates. He was recognized as an important personage in the *gubernia*. The order of Saint Vladimir and the rank of civil counselor brought the former townsman hereditary nobility. In the innumerable police questionnaires right up to 1917, his sons and daughters had to write down in the proper space their noble rank. But there was nothing aristocratic in the physical molds of either himself or the members of his family. Wide noses, high cheekbones, and stubby fingers revealed their plebeian origin. . . .

Maria Alexandrovna came from a more affluent and cultivated family than her husband. Her father, a physician and owner of an estate in Kazan *gubernia*, was married to a German woman who reared her children in German traditions. . . .

What little we know of the parents justifies the conclusion that the mother was of a higher spiritual quality than the father. From her issued those invisible rays that warm the heart of a child and give him a sense of warmth throughout his life. She did not caress her children impetuously and kiss them to death, but she also never pushed them away, never lit into them. From their first day she surrounded them with self-sacrificing love—without pampering but also without nagging. . . .

Were there not in this world such generous women, life itself would not deserve the name. Maria Alexandrovna found an active external expression for her precious powers only through her children. She lived to almost within a year of her son's historic victory.

Born and reared in a family that was not of the Russian Orthodox faith, Maria Alexandrovna, although wholly Russified, nevertheless possessed, in contrast to her husband, no firm church traditions—except indeed for the German Christmas tree—and was not distinguished in the least by religious observance. But Maria Alexandrovna never broke with religion entirely; in the most trying moments she resorted to it with all the hidden passion of her nature. Once, when the life of her four-year-old son hung by a thread, the mother, frantic with grief, whispered feverishly to her six-year-old daughter: "Pray for Sasha [Lenin's gifted older brother, Alexander]!" And she herself fell to her knees before the icon in despair. That time the danger passed. Seventeen years later—after how many alarms and labors and hopes!—through the bars of a Petersburg prison, the mother repeated to her daughter the same admonition: "Pray for Sasha!" But this time she spoke only of the saving of his soul, for the czar's noose had already strangled her beloved eldest son, the pride and hope of the family. . . .

[*On March 1, 1887, Alexander, an intense, idealistic young biology student at St. Petersburg University, joined four*

In this family portrait of 1879 nine-year-old Vladimir Ulyanov—later Lenin—sits at right. His mother (with baby Maria) and father are also seated, as is young Dimitri in the center. Standing (left to right) are Olga, Alexander, and Anna.

other students in an abortive attempt to assassinate Czar Alexander III. Alexander's deed, his execution, and the disgrace it brought to the Ulyanovs would mark the turning point in the placid, conventional life of the young Lenin-to-be.]

In the fourteen years from 1864 to 1878 the Ulyanovs had seven children. If you omit the fifth, Nikolai, who lived only a few days, the data we possess permits an instructive conclusion. The outstanding children in both character and ability—Alexander, Vladimir, and Olga—constitute the middle-age group, with Vladimir occupying the central place. The eldest daughter, Anna, and the two younger members of the family, although possessing many admirable qualities, hardly rose above the average level. At Vladimir's birth the father was thirty-nine and the mother thirty-five—the age of complete bloom of physical and spiritual forces. . . .

Volodya [diminutive of Vladimir] learned to walk late—almost at the same time as his little sister Olya [Olga], who was a year and a half younger. His first achievements in this activity were not altogether happy. He fell often and heavily and moreover on his head, so that the neighbors could always accurately calculate his orbit. "Probably his head was too heavy," writes his sister. With every fall Volodya would fill the entire house with his screaming. In those early years he seldom missed an opportunity to develop his vocal chords. "The passion for destruction," said Bakunin, who died in exile when the future Lenin was six years old, "is a creative passion." Volodya was an unqualified adherent of this formula. He destroyed his toys before ever beginning to play with them. Upon receiving from his nurse the gift of a sleigh with three horses made out of cardboard, he hid behind the door to escape annoying interference from adults and twisted the horses' legs until they came off.

His independent and passionate character expressed itself, it seems, very early. Adults were often compelled to

Elder brother Alexander Ulyanov

call this noisy and boisterous boy to order. "You mustn't yell so loud on a steamboat," said his mother as they sailed away for a summer in Kazan province. "But the steamboat is yelling loud himself," answered Volodya without lowering his voice. . . .

Sasha was inventive in games but restrained even in his favorites. Volodya was endlessly wanting to "catch up and overtake" everybody and did not mind using his elbows to this end. In many other respects Volodya differed even in early childhood from his elder brother. Sasha was patient and loved to collect things and do scrollwork with a saw, thus perfecting the attention and patience of the future biologist. Volodya had no use for painstaking pastimes. One time when Sasha was sorting theatrical handbills and carefully spreading them out on the floor, little Volodya jumped on the precious colored sheets, stamping, messing them up, and tearing some. Sasha could not comprehend such barbarism. . . .

Sasha was organically and almost morbidly truthful. To trick people and to tell lies was as unthinkable to him as to mock and scold. In difficult situations he remained silent. In the healthy truthfulness of Voloyda there was an element of slyness. With the overflowing, expansive force of such a nature as his, it was impossible to get along without some defensive lies. One could not, for instance, enjoy an apple peel without picking it up on the sly when a vigilant mother had left the kitchen; one could not tear the legs off a paper horse without hiding behind the door. And could one think

of confessing to an aunt, a relative stranger, that it was he, Volodya, who had broken the carafe while running through the rooms during a visit to her house? . . .

In 1878, when Volodya was eight years old, the Ulyanovs moved into a house of their own. It was made of wood and modest, but it had an orchard that became an object of care and concern to the entire family. The children were accurately informed about which bushes and trees were for them and which for the winter storage or for their father's name day, and they all observed a strict discipline of enjoyment. A little girl visitor once playfully bit a piece out of an apple right on the tree, and then ran away. A half a century later Anna Yelizarova remembered this catastrophe: "Such hooliganism (!) was alien and incomprehensible to us." This judgment, astonishing in its pedantry, sheds pretty good light on the patriarchal ways of that family, where discipline was enforced in different ways, but with great success, by both father and mother. Thrift, orderliness, respect for labor and its fruits, were learned early in life by the great destroyer of the future. Though he himself would not, of course, have called an innocent childish prank "hooliganism," he came to dislike slovenliness and extravagance among adults. . . .

At the age of nine and a half Volodya entered the first class at high school. Now he wore a uniform "like Sasha," and was subject to the authority of the same teachers, also uniformed, with double-headed eagles on their metal buttons. But Volodya's personality allowed him to endure far more easily then Alexander the high-school regime, with its hypocrisy and coercion. Even classicism was no burden to him. The future writer and public speaker early developed a taste for the ancient authors. Vladimir learned with extraordinary ease. This active and noisy boy, with his wide scope of emotions, was also capable of truly astounding concentration. Sitting motionless behind his desk, he would seize and absorb every explanation made by his teachers, so that a lesson assigned was for him a lesson learned. At home, he would quickly finish the next day's assignment. While the two older children spread out their books on the big table in the dining room, Volodya would begin his active life: noisemaking, chattering, and teasing the younger children. The older sister and brother would protest. The mother's authority would not always be sufficient. Volodya would turn up everywhere. Sometimes the father, if at home, would take his "jack-in-the-box" to his study to find out whether he really had finished his lessons. But Volodya would give all the answers without hesitation. The father would then take his old notebooks and quiz him on the entire course. Volodya was still invulnerable. Latin words were firmly engraved in his memory. The father did not know whether to be happy or upset. The boy learned too fast, and would perhaps fail to develop systematic work habits.

On returning home from school, Volodya would report to his parents the events of the day—chiefly what subjects he was called up on and how he answered. Since his progress was rather monotonous, this report would take the form of a swift run past his father's office and a shout: "5 in Greek, 5 in German." On the next day, and the day after: "5 in Latin, 5 in algebra." The father and mother would exchange secret smiles of satisfaction. Ilya Nikolayevich did not like to praise his children to their faces, and especially this self-confident boy to whom everything came so easy. But their children's success introduced, of course, a joyful note into the family life. In the evenings they would all gather happily round the big tea table. Ilya Nikolayevich never lost his taste for jokes and school anecdotes. There was much laughter, and the ringleader of it all was often the superintendent of schools. "You felt warm and cozy in that friendly family," related the teacher Kashkadamova. "Keenest of all in con-

The future Lenin, aged seventeen

versation were Volodya and his second sister, Olya. How their happy voices and infectious laughter would ring out!" . . .

There was a chess set in the house, whittled by the father in Nizhni Novgorod, which had gradually become a family heirloom of sorts. The male members of the family, beginning with the father, were devoted to the abstract intricacies of this ancient game—a game in which superiority in certain (to be sure, not very high) intellectual qualities finds a most direct expression and satisfaction. The sons always responded joyfully to a challenge from the father to play a game of chess. But the balance of power increasingly shifted to the younger generation. Alexander got hold of a textbook on chess, and with his usual calm persistence plunged into the theory of the game. After a while Vladimir followed him. The brothers evidently progressed alarmingly, for one evening, as he was going upstairs, Vladimir ran into his father filching the textbook from the attic with the obvious aim of arming himself for future battles.

But as the proverb goes, an hour for fun, and time itself for work. Vladimir climbed the steps of his high-school curricula without pause and each year with prizes. Only in the seventh grade did he run into trouble with his French teacher, an ignorant and shifty individual who then became a target for his mockery. His recklessness was punished: the Frenchman managed to get the prize pupil marked down one grade in conduct for the semester. Ilya Nikolayevich was ruffled, and Vladimir

solemnly promised to put an end to these risky experiments. The incident had no consequences. Behind this insolence toward a disrespected teacher the school authorities discovered no dangerous turn of mind. And they were not mistaken—for the time being. . . .

Vladimir became famous in the class as a "literary man." The verbal timidity of Alexander was completely alien to him. That sturdy and aggressive self-confidence that alarmed his father, and must on occasion have been distasteful to the elder brother, remained with Vladimir in creative writing as well. When he sat down to write a composition—never at the last moment, but in good time—he knew in advance that he would say all that was necessary and say it right. Picking out a hard pencil and sharpening it well, that the letters might lie fine and compact on the paper, he would first of all sketch out an outline, so as to make sure that all his ideas would be expressed in full. Around this outline he would then group references and quotations—not only from school texts, but from other books as well. With this preparatory work finished, the references numbered, and the introduction and conclusions mapped out, the composition very nearly wrote itself. It remained only to carefully write out a clean copy. His language and literature teacher, Kerensky,* who was also the school principal, greatly favored this sturdy redheaded composition writer, and would set up his writings as an example to the others . . .

The name of Marx meant nothing to this young man whose interests lay almost exclusively in belles-lettres. He gave himself up to literature with a passion. For whole days he drank in the novels of Turgenev, page by page, lying on his cot carried away into the realm of "superfluous people" and idealized maidens under the linden trees of aristocratic parks. Having read through to the end he would begin all over again. His thirst was insatiable. . . .

Although Vladimir fell ill occasionally during his school years, he was of

*Fyodor Kerensky, the father of Alexander Kerensky (1881–1970), the future prime minister of the democratic provisional government that was deposed as a result of Lenin's *coup d'état* of November 7, 1917

reasonably sturdy health and his body matured satisfactorily. With his abilities there could be no problem of an excessive expenditure of energy. He grew like a young oak, putting down deep roots and drinking in abundantly the air and moisture. What can one say but—"a happy childhood"?

The Ulyanov family had lived a happy life for almost twenty-three years and had been like other harmonious and fortunate families. In 1886 the first blow fell, the death of the father. . . . He had fallen sick in January, while preparing his annual report. Alexander was in Petersburg, wholly immersed in his zoology term paper. Vladimir, only a year and a half away from high-school graduation, must have been thinking already about the university. Anna was at home for the Christmas holidays. Neither the family nor the physician took Ilya Nikolayevich's illness seriously. He continued to work on his report. His daughter sat reading some papers to him until she noticed that her father was becoming delirious. The next morning, January 12, the sick man did not come to the table, but only to the dining-room door, looking in "as though he had come to say good-bye," remembered Maria Alexandrovna. At five o'clock the mother, in alarm, called Anna and Vladimir. Ilya Nikolayevich lay dying on the sofa that served him for a bed. The children saw their father shudder twice and become still forever. He was not yet fifty-five years old. . . .

Anna remained in Simbirsk for a while in order to be near her mother. It was at that time that the elder sister and Vladimir grew close to each other. There were winter walks and long conversations in which the brother revealed himself to Anna as a rebel and a nonconformist, the embodiment of protest—so far, however, only in relation to "the school authorities, high-school studies, and also to religion." During the summer vacation these moods had not yet existed.

The death of the father had suddenly destroyed the lulling flow of life in a family whose well-being had seemed sure to go on indefinitely. How can we avoid assuming that it was this blow that imparted a new critical direction to Vladimir's thoughts? . . .

Recovering comparatively soon after the death of his father, Vladimir felt himself the man in the family. His recent emancipation from religion must have suddenly elevated his self-esteem. As often happens with headstrong youths, the need for independence took a rough and tough form in him in that critical period—at the expense of others, and in particular, at the expense of his mother's authority. "Mockery was natural to Vladimir in general, and, at that transitional age, especially so." We can rely on these words the more surely since the elder sister, as she is portrayed in her own writing, would not easily have forgotten these mockeries. As for Alexander, he was painfully sensitive to gibes at the expense of others, and it would never occur to anyone to sneer at Alexander himself. He first came into contact with this in the summer spent with the fatherless family. Each brother was now tuned to a different key. The phase of childish worship, when Volodya wanted to do everything "like Sasha," had given way to a struggle for independence; the inevitable rejection of his elder brother had begun. His concentration, his attentiveness to other people, his fear of revealing his superiority, Vladimir offset with a noisy aggressiveness, sneering, gibes, and an organic desire to dominate. The summer passed in disharmony.

Let us listen to Anna Yelizarova. Volodya's abruptness and aggressiveness "became especially noticeable after the death of the father, whose presence had always had a restraining effect upon the boys." Vladimir began to "talk back to his mother, sometimes harshly, as he would never have dared while Father was with us." Perhaps this demonstrative impudence of Vladimir's was also, in a way, a retroactive protest against the father's authoritarianism. The mother subsequently remembered with emotion how Sasha had sometimes interceded in her behalf during that last summer. Once, while playing chess, Vladimir carelessly waved away his mother's reminder about some task, and when Maria Alexandrovna insisted with some irritation, he answered with a wisecrack. Then Alexander intervened: "Either you will do immediately what mama tells you or I won't play with you any longer." The ultimatum was presented calmly but so firmly that Vladimir immediately did as he was told. Anna herself, although she was annoyed at the "sneers, impertinence, and arrogance" of Volodya, nevertheless fell under his influence, or at any rate willingly kept up a chatter with him full of jokes, digs, and laughter. Alexander not only did not join in these conversations but found it difficult to tolerate them. He had his own moods, and Anna more than once brought upon herself his reproving looks. In the autumn, when they were in St. Petersburg, she summoned up the courage to put a question to Sasha: "How do you like our Volodya?" Sasha answered: "Undoubtedly a very able person, but we don't get along." . . .

Henceforth the family would have to live on the mother's pension, pieced out perhaps with some small savings the father had left. They crowded themselves a little and took in boarders. But the regimen of life remained the same. Maria Alexandrovna watched over the younger children, and waited for the oldest to graduate from the university. They all worked hard. Vladimir delighted her with his successes but alarmed her with his arrogance. So passed the year of mourning. Life was beginning to move again in its new, narrower channel, when a second blow —a double blow at that—descended on the family: both son and daughter were involved in a trial for an attempted assassination of the czar.

Anna was arrested on March 1 in her brother's rooms in St. Petersburg, which she had entered while a search was in progress. Shrouded in dreadful uncertainty, the girl was locked up in prison in connection with a case in which she had had no part. This, then, is what Sasha was busy with! . . .

A Petersburg relative of the Ulyanovs wrote of the arrest of Alexander and Anna to a former teacher of the children asking her to prepare the mother. Narrowing his young brows, Vladimir stood silent a long time over the Petersburg letter. This lightning stroke revealed the figure of Alexander in a new light. "But this is a serious thing," he said. "It may end badly for Sasha." He evidently had no doubt of Anna's innocence. The task of preparing his mother fell to him. But, sensing tragedy in his first words, she demanded the letter and immediately made ready for a journey.

There was still no railroad from Simbirsk; one had to travel by horse and wagon to Syzran. For the sake of economy and for safety on the journey, Vladimir sought a companion for his mother. But the news had already spread through the town. Everyone turned away fearfully. No one would travel with the mother of a terrorist. Vladimir never forgot this lesson. The days that followed were to mean much in the forming of his character and its direction. The youth became austere and silent, and frequently shut himself up in his room when he was not busy with the younger children left in his charge. So *that* is what he was, this tireless chemist and dissector of worms, this silent brother so near and yet so unknown! When compelled to speak with Kashkadamova of the catastrophe, he kept repeating: "It means Alexander could not have acted otherwise." The mother came back for a short time to see the children and told them of her efforts and her hope of a life sentence to hard labor for Sasha. "In that case I would go with him," she said. "The older children are big enough and I will take the younger with me." Instead of a chair at a university and scholarly glory, chains and

Triumphant Bolshevik, Lenin in 1919 stands between Stalin, at left, Russia's future dictator, and Trotsky, Stalin's future victim.

stripes now became the chief object of the mother's hopes. . . .

On the eve of the execution, still hoping, she kept repeating to her son through the double grating: "Have courage!" On May 5, on her way to an interview with her daughter, she learned from a leaflet passed out in the street that Sasha was no more. . . .

Simbirsk was fragrant with all the flowers of its orchards when news came from the capital of the hanging of Alexander Ulyanov. The family of a full state counselor, until then respected on every side, became overnight the family of an executed state criminal. Friends and acquaintances, without exception, avoided the house on Moscow Street. Even the aged schoolteacher who had so often dropped in for a game of chess with Ilya Nikolayevich, no longer showed his face. . . .

Some years later the Social Democrat Lalayants questioned Lenin about the affair of March 1. Lenin answered: "Alexander's participation in a terrorist act was completely unexpected for all of us. Possibly my sister knew something—I knew nothing at all."

Lenin's grief for his brother must have been colored with bitterness at the thought that Alexander had concealed from him his deepest and most important thoughts, and with remorse over his own lack of attentiveness toward his brother and his arrogant assertions of his own independence. His childish worship of Sasha must have returned now with tenfold strength, sharpened by feelings of guilt and a consciousness of the impossibility of making amends. The teacher who handed him the fateful letter from St. Petersburg says: "Before me sat

no longer the carefree cheerful boy but a grown man buried in thought . . ."

Vladimir went through his final high-school experiences with his teeth clenched. There exists a photograph, evidently made for the high-school diploma. On the still unformed but strongly concentrated features with the arrogantly pushed out lower lip lay the shadow of grief and of a first deep hatred. Two deaths stood at the beginning of the new period of Vladimir's life. The death of his father, convincing in its physiological naturalness, impelled him to a critical attitude toward the church and the religious myth. The execution of his brother awakened bitter hostility toward the hangmen. The future revolutionary had been planted in the personality of the youth and in the social conditions that formed him. But an initial impulse was needed. And this was provided by the unexpected death of his brother. The first political thoughts of Vladimir must inevitably have arisen out of a twofold need: to avenge Sasha and to refute by action Sasha's distrust. . . . But calls to battle were nowhere to be heard. Vladimir knew not how to approach the task of revenge.

• • •

[*Anna was released from prison a few days after Alexander was hanged. A few weeks later Vladimir was graduated from the Simbirsk high school with honors as its best student. With Kerensky testifying to his respectable and reliable ways, Vladimir entered the Kazan university with the intention of studying law. Bearing the now infamous name of Ulyanov and watched by the czarist police, he was expelled from the university that December for taking part in a student demonstration. After that Lenin studied law—and the writings of Karl Marx—on his own; he passed the examination in 1891, and even practiced law in St. Petersburg for a time. By 1895, however, Lenin's commitment to revolutionary politics had eclipsed his last residual concern for a respectable career.*]

mer. For the moment, the cheering men of Flers drowned the rising volume of criticism and persuaded the public that encores were needed. Not for nothing were thousands of families receiving their packets of last effects, which sometimes included shreds of a bloody uniform suitable for burying in the back garden. Possibly the bereaved at home would not have been heartened had they known that the "cheering army" behind the tank (how relentlessly the press applied its magnifying glass to the event) was only a batch of German prisoners being formed up.

The lengthening casualty lists of the Somme seemed to touch everyone. At the beginning of September the Liberal Prime Minister, Herbert Asquith, went to see the battlefield for himself. He inspected the "caterpillars," drank rather too much of Haig's old brandy (Haig thought), and urged the commander in chief not to dissipate the surprise in local attacks. One lovely hot day near Fricourt, Asquith met his eldest son, Raymond, who was waiting on horseback at a crossroads. Raymond, though overaged for a subaltern at thirty-eight, was yet the model of the New Army volunteer: aloofly handsome, a family man, and a barrister, whose sharp wit and general gifts marked him for greater things. The Prime Minister found his son looking "so radiantly strong and confident that I came away from France with an easier mind."

Raymond Asquith was mortally wounded leading the first wave of the September 15 attack. "One might have known that nothing so brilliant and precious could escape," his brother's wife, Lady Cynthia Asquith, wrote in her diary. "Now I feel I have really relinquished all hope and expect no one to survive. . . . all our intellect is being chucked away in the trenches." The Prime Minister was inconsolable. "Whatever pride I had in the past," he wrote on September 20, "and whatever hope I had for the far future—by much the largest part of both was invested in him. Now all that is gone. It will take me a few days more to get back my

bearings." As Asquith's biographer Roy Jenkins notes, it took him much longer than that. He grew uncommunicative, skipped Cabinet meetings, and only by an effort of will did he get through a Parliamentary speech in mid-October. Meanwhile, Lloyd George had initiated his behind-the-scenes campaign against Asquith. The old man was clearly no longer up to a struggle for power, and the events on the Somme did not strengthen his position. In December, after nine years as Prime Minister, he resigned. Lloyd George formed a new government.

Raymond Asquith died in a field hospital during the night of September 15, and it may have been that the final earthly sound he heard was the tattoo of rain overhead. As squalls swept the darkened battlefield, Haig's last bid for a breakout subsided into the mud like a derelict tank (how many of them there were now). But the Somme, and the Somme rains, continued. They fought, says the Official History, "up to the waist in slime," and had to pull each other out as they advanced. Thiepval and Schwaben Redoubt fell, and the British took over ground still covered by the dead of July 1. Intelligence reports had convinced Haig that the enemy was ready to give way, if only suitable pressure could be maintained—and, in fact, not until the end of the war would the Germans on the Western Front again experience such a dangerous manpower crisis. The mud became their ally, as it became the chief enemy of the British. Roads dissolved into deep slime, food and ammunition had to be dragged forward on sledges improvised from sheets of corrugated iron, and horses and mules sank to their bellies and had to be shot. The "dry places" that ration parties used as stepping stones often proved to be corpses—as Edmund Blunden remembered, "Those bemired carcasses . . . have not yet ceased to serve 'the great adventure.'"

Let us follow a battalion on its way to the line one night toward the end of

October. The last road has disappeared into the quagmire, and the men trudge in single file along a duckboard track that extends across the plain toward the quivering glow of Very lights and explosions illuminating the front. Water-filled shell holes crowd the landscape, their myriad surfaces capturing cold fragments of moonlight. At every hand the earth seems to spew up relics of the autumn's events, like a gigantic indigestion of history: a pile of rubble where a village stood, shredded stumps of trees, and bodies, unburied bodies everywhere, their useless gear heaped around them. A shell plops in the mud, someone goes down, but the line merely edges around him; this is no place to linger. Then the duckboards end, and the battalion passes over a brief ridge, miraculously still covered with grass. At the bottom of the hill a man shouts that he is up to his knees in mud. They have arrived.

The trench, little more than a hastily thrown-up dike, is empty: whoever they were supposed to relieve has gone already. James Lockhead Jack, a Scottish colonel commanding a West Yorkshire battalion, noted in his diary entry of October 24 that his men had carried out a relief in "persistent rain, deep mud, shell fire and bullets." There are few more quietly harrowing accounts of the sullen winding-down of the Somme than his, with its record of an exhaustion that was overtaking both sides.

October 25: The weather has become worse. . . . One patrol . . . captured 16 prisoners, who say they would have surrendered earlier but their sergeant—evidently a hard-hearted man—would not allow it.

We have lost today 3 officers and 41 other ranks . . . nearly all from shellfire.

October 26: . . . There are no dugouts in the forward area. . . . Officers and men have no cover from the fearful weather except their waterproof sheets rigged up in the trenches to form roofs. . . . The battalion casualties today number 30, chiefly to carrying parties and to support companies. I am quite sick with wondering how to obviate further losses . . .

Their hardships did not end with their relief on the eighth day; Jack and his men had to march back five miles at night. He was a Regular Army officer who had seen the worst the war could offer, including the slaughter of July 1, and he was not disposed to open emotion. But when he visited with his men the next day, he admitted that "I can scarcely keep sufficiently composed to say a few words to the gaunt, exhausted, patient lads."

But the duckboards could lead to an even more surreal conclusion. On September 15 Haig's troops had captured Le Sars, a single street of brick astride the Roman road. Beyond the village, the road dips into a broad depression and then starts gradually over the final ridge before Bapaume, now only three miles away. The more that chimera tantalized, the more elusive it seemed to grow; in the next two months Haig managed to nudge his reluctant line another four or five hundred yards down the forward slope.

This "new valley of humiliation," as Charles Carrington described it, was dominated by a man-made monstrosity, an ancient burial mound that the locals called the Butte de Warlencourt. "What Gallic chieftain slain by Caesar in the land of the Ambiani lay beneath this tumulus we cared not," he wrote. When the British had first caught sight of the Butte in September, it was still green, but by now all vegetation had been blown away, and it rose out of the mud, a gleaming, pock-marked dome of chalk perhaps sixty feet high. The terror of the machine guns that fired down from the slopes was probably imaginary, but it was an inhibiting terror nevertheless. "That ghastly hill, never free from the smoke of bursting shells, became fabulous," Carrington wrote. "It shone white in the night and seemed to leer at you like an ogre in a fairy tale. It loomed up unexpectedly, peering into trenches where you thought yourself safe: it haunted your dreams."

Bogged down: Mud engulfs horses pulling an ammunition limber.

He spent a total of fifteen days and nights under the Butte, an experience that left him "a nervous wreck," though he never glimpsed a German soldier.

How odd, how appropriate, that the British advance should spend itself before this death's-head, a place already haunted in its benign aspect. Its capture possessed them, out of all proportion to its real worth: the Germans probably used the Butte for observation only. Like men bent on snatching the prize from the top of a glass mountain, the British refused to give up.

Three understrength battalions of the Durham Light Infantry made the last serious attempt in a morning downpour on Sunday, November 5. Nothing seemed to go right. There was a moment in the day-long battle, though, when men of the mired battalions looked up and saw the solitary figure of a British soldier on the summit of the Butte. He paused, as if awaiting some sunlit signal of apotheosis, and then passed down out of sight. One battalion clung to the Butte until nightfall, but reinforcements, if any were available, never arrived, and around midnight the Durhams withdrew to their original lines. In a contest between somnambulists, who dreams about winning?

In the mid-1960's when an elderly Charles Carrington motored past, he was astonished to find "what an ordinary inconspicuous little mound" the Butte was. Fifty years had done their

work. Certainly I had expected something more dramatic than a tree-covered hummock at the crest of a low plateau—and yet, as I found when I visited it, the place had not lost its power to haunt.

The day itself was unsettling, the chilly July sky empty one minute and splattered with rain clouds the next. The climb through a wheat field to the Butte was deceptively steep and, even on firm ground, more tiring than it had any right to be—that fact alone told a good deal about the nature of the fighting here. Blundering about, I felt oddly menaced, as if at any moment I would set my foot too heavily on a buried shell and be blown up. That King George V himself had gone up the side of the Butte in 1917 hardly mattered: it *was* a creepy place.

A rough path emerged, though, and I followed it, skirting someone's recent excavation—a salvaged brass shell head, as I learned, can bring a franc or two, and a helmet is a treasure. Finally, just below the top, I had to grab a sapling and pull myself up. Except for a covering of briar and clumps of brown grass that made for treacherous footing, the summit of the Butte was bare, permanently tonsured by fire, I suppose. Over in one corner, by the edge of the trees, stood the only indication that something might once have happened—a weather-beaten wooden cross rising from a concrete pedestal. I returned by the route I had come. This time, at the bottom, I took a different way out. As I ducked under a branch, I saw in the grass by my foot a rusted hand grenade.

How do you disentangle the meaning of this place from fifty years' growth of hawthorn? I walked out into the fields, expecting not an answer but a better look. The Butte de Warlencourt really was an ordinary, inconspicuous little mound. On October 7, 1916, this part of the line was held by the German 16th Bavarian

Reserve Regiment. That was the day the British made their first serious attempt to reach the Butte, and the Bavarians stopped them at places with names like snag trench, the nose, and the pimple. It must have been somewhere out here that a shell fragment hit one of the Bavarian dispatch runners in the left thigh. His name was Adolf Hitler.

You can almost chart the progress of the war in its casual exclamations. Sir Edward Grey's remark in August, 1914, about the lamps going out all over Europe had become, by November, 1916, the last words spoken by H. H. Munro (Saki): "Put that bloody cigarette out." None would ever be lit again in his lifetime. Lance Sergeant Munro of the Royal Fusiliers, the fashionable author of O. Henryish tales who had chosen to bury himself in the ranks, was shot moments later in a crater near Beaumont Hamel. He was perhaps the most notable literary casualty of the Great War in his own time.

Munro's battalion took part in the last official action of the Somme campaign, an offensive set piece along the Ancre front between November 13 and 18 that caught the Germans off guard: given the condition of the terrain and the time of year, further attacks had seemed inconceivable. They obviously had not reckoned on the tenacity of the enemy high command. Though the British managed to advance the line as much as two miles, they still fell short of the objectives of July 1 in this sector. The battle of the Somme, which had begun in the pleasant sunshine of one morning, ended in the snow and darkness of another, with the indistinct figures of the infantry groping their way forward yet one more time over the white ground.

Do we judge the Somme by this final image? Almost any conclusion about it invites challenge or contra-

Aftermath: In 1917 a soldier surveys what once was Pozières. A derelict British tank can be seen in the background at the right.

diction. Let us forget the debate over casualties immediately: you can prove anything you want according to what set of statistics you choose. If the Allies did not achieve their breakthrough, did stalemate constitute defeat? Which do we weigh more heavily: the slaughter of the first day and the missed opportunities of the 140 following, or the increasing desperation of the defenders? If the process of attrition hardly provided a stirring advertisement for itself, did its dim benefits nevertheless vindicate the principle? Who did win in the end? Or rather, who could least afford what he lost?

On that score, the decision must go to the Allies, narrowly and on points. Their losses, in a strictly military sense, were not irreplaceable; those of the enemy were. The old, highly trained core of the German infantry disappeared on the Somme. The battle was, as a Captain von Hentig wrote, "the muddy grave of the German field army, and of the faith in the infallibility of the German leaders, dug by British industry and its shells." His verdict is echoed again and again. The Germans had lost the most important battle of all, the one they contemptuously referred to as the material battle. "The German Supreme Command, which entered the war with enormous superi-

ority had fallen behind in the application of destructive forces, and was compelled to throw division after division without protection against them into the cauldron of the battle of annihilation." Industry prevailed where men could only endure—that is the lesson of the Somme, as it is of all conventional modern wars.

Back in September, after the Hindenburg–Ludendorff partnership had taken over the German Supreme Command, they had ordered the building of a vast and sophisticated trench system far to the rear of the Somme battlefield. It was only thought of as a precautionary measure at the time, but by midwinter—the worst in twenty years—the prospect of retirement could no longer be put off. The Germans retreated to their new positions, which the British called the Hindenburg Line, leaving a desert in their wake. Ironically, the Allied infantry and cavalry had become so accustomed to the French stalemate, and were so bewildered by their first taste of open warfare, that they let the enemy slip clean away. You can either take the German retreat as a move of brilliance—by shortening his line, Ludendorff conserved thirteen or fourteen divisions—or as an admission of defeat. It was a little of both. As the British advanced, at last taking possession of the Butte of Warlencourt and the burned-out shell of Bapaume, they noticed a sign erected on the town hall of a nearby village: "Don't be angry, only wonder!"

What better epitaph for the Somme —or, indeed, for any buried trauma? "I felt that this war had made the past seem very peculiar," Siegfried Sassoon reflected, convalescing in an Oxford hospital that summer. "People weren't the same as they used to be, or else I had changed. Was it that I had experienced something that they couldn't share or imagine?" He watched a tall man with a neatly trimmed beard "pushing his son very slowly across the lawn in a long wheeled bed." Pausing in the shade, the father read him Haig's latest dispatch. The boy said nothing. He had lost a leg on July 1.

As I write, I can't help thinking of a different summer scene. It is a photograph made about 1910, give or take a couple of years, and it shows a group of young men and women picnicking somewhere in the English countryside. The whole tableau has the look of a bank-holiday outing. The women wear the kind of flowered picture hats that are reserved for such occasions; the men, clerks and apprentices probably, and scarcely more than boys, pose around the white cloth in exaggerated attitudes of relaxation. One stretches out in the tall grass, his eyes closed and a cigar clenched between his teeth, his head resting on the knees of a girl who is trying to suppress a giggle. Another young man turns away in a diffidently smiling blur, as intrigued by the girls as by the camera. Ties are loosened. A claret bottle stands empty. Nailed to a line of trees receding behing them is a single strand of barbed wire. Did these same men, I wonder, rush together to join one of the Pals battalions in 1914? Did some of them plod forward at 7:30 A.M. on July 1, a day very like this? Did I pass by their graves?

"So ends the golden age," mourned the official historian of the 9th Yorks and Lancs, a New Army battalion that lost 423 men that day. The phrase may be hyperbole, but the sense of having experienced a trauma of historical proportions is real enough. For England, the phenomenon we think of as the nineteenth century may be Anchored Safe on those gusty ridges, Gone but Not Forgotten. "From this frightful forfeit dates the decline of the West," another historian would write forty-odd years later. He is the twentieth century speaking, and whether you agree with him or not is really beside the point. Perhaps we all did lose a little at the Somme—perhaps that is why the image of an Edwardian picnic continues to haunt me. I understand better now what Fitzgerald's character Dick Diver meant when he said, in *Tender is the Night,* that battles like the Somme were "invented by Lewis Carroll and Jules Verne and whoever wrote Undine, and country deacons bowling and marraines in Marseilles and girls seduced in the back lanes of Würtemberg and Westphalia. Why, this was a love battle—there was a century of middle-class love spent here. This was the last love battle."

He was standing in a bit of neat restored trench—still preserved as a monument—where the Newfoundland battalion lost 684 out of some 800 men on July 1. "In front of him beneath a dingy sky was Beaumont Hamel, to his left the tragic hill of Thiepval." It was characteristic that Fitzgerald, whose sense of history was impeccable, still managed to get his directions reversed.

There was a time between the wars when busloads of people would stop at the Somme; almost no one does any more. A few regulars show up, like the old soldier who makes a point of standing, at 7:30 A.M. sharp on July 1, on the exact spot where he went over the top. One small bit of trench, the same one that Dick Diver visited, remains as a tourist attraction. You may wander through the original bays and traverses, pick up the rim of a helmet or a harmless bit of shell, and glance down the hill to the German trenches two hundred yards away. The iron wire holders with their twin loops still rise from the grass, but the wire itself was removed a few years ago: too many sheep were getting caught in it.

As many as ten bodies a year are still uncovered, and like archaeologists, the Commonwealth War Graves people sift the earth around the bones in the hopes of finding a regimental badge with a serial number. By 1971 they had accounted for 1,002 of the 73,077 names on the Thiepval monument.

Wandering one morning over those old battlefields, I met the supervisor of the Heilly Station Military Cemetery. Heilly, a pretty village on the Ancre, a tributary of the Somme, was ten miles behind the front in 1916, but two years later, when the Germans drove the Allies back forty miles in little more than a week, their advance stalled just over the hill from the cemetery. As we talked, a black steam locomotive appeared, belching thick clouds of white smoke as it chuffed its way along the line of poplars that hid the Ancre River from view. It stopped at the Heilly station, a yellow stucco building with a red tile roof that could have come straight out of a Magritte painting. The supervisor remarked that in 1916 a hospital had occupied the field by the station.

Robert Graves was brought there after he had been hit by fragments of a German shell. Graves's colonel saw him lying unconscious in a corner of a dressing station and was told that he wouldn't survive the night. The colonel went back to write a letter of condolence to the boy's mother. But the next morning, clearing away the dead, medical orderlies found him still alive and put his shattered body on an ambulance for Heilly. "Close to the station," Graves remembered, "stood the hospital tents with the red cross prominently painted on the roofs, to discourage air-bombing. Fine July weather made the tents insufferably hot. I was semi-conscious now, and aware of my lung-wound owing to a shortness of breath. It amused me to watch the little bubbles of blood, like scarlet soap-bubbles, which my breath made in escaping through the opening of my wound . . ."

I once spent a summer in the Majorcan village where Graves still lives, its most conspicuous citizen. He used to sit on the beach in the afternoons surrounded, not unwillingly, by admirers, a flamboyant old man in a floppy hat. At some point he would always climb the rocks and dive into the sea. How do you reconcile that sight with an empty field by a railroad station—a station where nobody gets off and nobody gets on, in a world made safe for the democracy of the dead?

Hwang it all—which Wong are you?

HORIZON submits the names of our political leaders to the acid test of the Chinese ideograph

There are relatively few Chinese family names (not more than a hundred of them), and these family, or clan, names, written first and then followed by a given name, are used by all the seven or eight hundred million Chinese in the world. In the classical writings of China, the Chinese people are often referred to as the "Old Hundred Names."

When one of these names is written in English, it can be spelled in a variety of ways, such as Wu or Woo; Soong or Sung; Li or Lee; Chan or Chen; Mao or Mow; Wang, Wong, or Hwang; and the fascinating vowelless name of Ng or Eng. The same problem also exists in Chinese, and to resolve this dilemma of two names that sound the same but can be written differently, one asks, "How do you write (your) honorable (or precious) name?" In other words, "Which Wong are you—'The King' or 'Yellow'?" or "Are you the Lee of 'Beneficial' or of 'Plum Tree'?" The individual questioned thereupon writes out his family name or sketches it rapidly in his palm with a forefinger. Since there are only one hundred Chinese family names, the answer is immediately understood.

Whenever barbarians invaded or visited China in past centuries, the Chinese family names obviously did not apply to them. A phonetic rendition had to be made up, comprised of Chinese syllables (each syllable generally means something) that would sound vaguely like the foreign name, and if possible, be evocative and dignified. This is happening again now, when interest in America (called Mei-Kuo, literally "Beautiful Land,") has caused a new crop of names to be printed in the Chinese press.

President Nixon's name is written with the ideographs Ni-Ko-Sen, which translated means "Mud Overcomes Forest." Dr. Henry Kissinger's name, Chi-Hsin-Chia, breaks down to "Lucky Laborious (at) Home." If Governor Reagan were to visit China, his name might be written Lei-Ken, with ideographs meaning "Thunder Root" or "Root of the Thunder," while a usually more thunderous member of his political party, Vice-President Agnew, would find that his last name, An-Ku-Niu, has the sur-

prising meaning of "Peaceful Personality Knot."

Among opposition leaders, Senator Edmund Muskie's name, Mai-Ssu-Ki, translated as "Wheat Clever Basic," has a certain appeal to confidence and plenty, while Eugene McCarthy's, Ma-Ka-Hsi, or "Horse Cardboard Tin," makes a somewhat confusing picture. Senator Edward Kennedy's name, by an unusual coincidence, comes out Ken-Na-Ti, "Sweet Take World," a not so cryptic message to, or from, female and youthful voters.

Senator George McGovern, written Ma-Ko-Yuen, translates, appropriately, to "Wheat High Cloud"; Governor George Wallace, Hwa-Lai-Tsu, becomes "Flowery

Arriving Scholar," doubtless a reference to his stand at the schoolroom door; and Hubert H. Humphrey, Han-Fu-Li, means "Korea Prosperous Benefit." Vietnam prosperity was apparently never in the cards.

The usual characters chosen to express Governor Nelson Rockefeller's name, Lo-Ke-Fei-Le, mean "River Conquers Activity Prosperity," although a twist of a syllabic character would make it come out as "River Conquered Activity Chokes," perhaps a plea for a Hudson River expressway. Mayor John V. Lindsay's name, written Lin-Hsi, means "Forest West," but if a critic wished to slightly change the characters in this name to Lin-Tsei, it would approximate the same sound but would mean "Forest Robber" or "Bandit of the Woods," an allusion either to the municipal seizure of Central Park woodlands or to the current lack of security therein.

The slight modification of a character, while preserving its sound, has long been a medium of official Chinese insults. This is especially easy in a language where a single syllable can have more than forty different meanings, depending on how it is written. Recently, a Communist Party secretary, Li Hsueh-feng, found his name changed from "Snowy Mountaintop" to the equivalent of "Bloody Weirdo." Similarly, Fu Ch'ung-pi, an ex-commander of the Peking garrison, found his name subtly altered from "Magnificent Precious Stone" to "Corpse of Miserable Worm."

Frequently, while conserving the family name, given names are changed to prove a point. The word "Mao" can mean "cat," "feather," "hair," "counterfeit," "risk," or "cap." But in the name Mao Tse-tung, it means "hair" or "feather." In his youth, however, Mao changed his given name to Tse-tung, "Benefactor of the East." The "Chiang" of General Chiang Kai-shek's name is written as "general" with the sign for grass on top—to designate it as a family name, not to imply that grass is growing on the general.

A famous though somewhat grisly pun took its place in ancient Chinese history at the time of the emperor-dictator Chin Shih Huang-ti. This emperor, long infamous in Chinese annals because, in a one-man cultural revolution, he attempted to destroy all books and records written before his reign so that history would start with him, was also the unifier of China and the builder of the Great Wall. As the Great Wall was being built, the number of deaths among the construction levies increased to the point where a popular saying or prophecy was circulated that the Great Wall would never be finished unless ten thousand men were buried within it.

According to history, the resourceful emperor found a man whose name character, Wan, meant "Ten Thousand" and interred him forthwith in what the Chinese call "The Ten Thousand Mile Long Wall," thereby fulfilling at one stroke the prophecy and the ultimate success of his public works project, and establishing as well the importance of what one's name means in Chinese.

By CHARLES F. BERLITZ